# Psychology in Practice:
# Organisations

# PSYCHOLOGY
## in Practice

## Organisations

**Hugh Coolican**

Hodder & Stoughton
A MEMBER OF THE HODDER HEADLINE GROUP

Orders: please contact Bookpoint Ltd, 130 Milton Park, Abingdon, Oxon OX14 4SB. Telephone: (44) 01235 827720. Fax: (44) 01235 400454. Lines are open from 9.00 – 6.00, Monday to Saturday, with a 24 hour message answering service. Email address: orders@bodkpoint.co.uk

*British Library Cataloguing in Publication Data*
A catalogue record for this title is available from the British Library

ISBN 0 340 80416 5

First Published 2001
Impression number 10 9 8 7 6 5 4 3 2 1
Year 2007 2006 2005 2004 2003 2002 2001

Typeset by Dorchester Typesetting Group Limited, Dorset, England
Printed in Great Britain for Hodder & Stoughton Educational, a division of Hodder Headline Plc, 338 Euston Road, London NW1 3BH by The Bath Press Ltd.

# CONTENTS

# Introduction

You will probably spend around half of your waking life as a person behaving in an organisation. The organisations you act within include your school, your college and, later, the organisations that you work for. You may also act within voluntary organisations such as a football club, a self help group or a charitable organisation. Apart from being influenced by an organisation while we are actually within it, our behaviour is also influenced at a distance: we have to limit our activities to allow for travel to work, we bring work home, we may work from home part of the time, we discuss our attitudes to work with friends, we go out with work colleagues and form long-term relationships. Very many of us end up married to someone we met at college or work. In many ways we could say that much of our behaviour is influenced through organisations. Not surprisingly, then, the psychology of organisations is not so much an *application* of psychology but a *root* of many theories encountered in Social Psychology or the study of Individual Differences, a point expanded further below.

## What is organisational psychology?

Organisational Psychology is the study of organisations and of human behaviour within them. It includes the ways in which our behaviour is influenced by the formal and informal rules of the organisation, its principles, its communication networks and its structures. However it also includes the ways in which individuals and groups contribute to the functioning of the organisation and the ways in which the organisation as a whole performs and develops. The last phrase is emphasised because psychology, being largely a product of the USA and Western nations, tends to think in terms of the relationship between the individual and the organisation. In more *collectivist* societies such as Japan and India (see Triandis, 1994) individuals tend to see themselves *first* as part of a social group, e.g. the family, the company. Individual efforts are played down compared with the effort of the group or team as a whole. In the West there tends to be the conception of individuals working as single units for their own personal success. Hence organisations have tended to think in terms of how to *harness* individual aspirations and energy and how to *persuade* individuals to work as a team. Had organisational psychology grown up in the East, we might have quite a different set of theories and findings. The focus might have been more on the organisation rather than on the individuals that *make up* the organisation. Both these aspects are contained in this book but, since Western syllabuses emphasise the Western concept of the individual and the organisation, so does this book.

# Terminology

Let's first clear up some inevitable confusion with terms. In 1921 the self-financing National Institute of Industrial Psychology (NIIP) was established in Britain. The early name for the field then was **Industrial Psychology** but, by the 1950s, the term **Occupational Psychology** had become the more generally used term. This is currently the name of the appropriate division of the British Psychological Society (BPS). Recently members have debated a change of title towards the common European term, **Work Psychology**, but with no change as yet. In the UK, practising professionals are known as **Occupational Psychologists**. They are likely to have a Bachelor's degree in general psychology and a Masters' qualification in occupational psychology. Membership of the Occupational Psychology Division, along with supervised work practice, permits an application to the BPS to become a **Chartered Occupational Psychologist** and to use the letters C.Psychol. after one's name. The term **Work and Organisational Psychology** is also often used in the UK to describe the field and appears on several undergraduate and postgraduate courses. In the USA the term **Industrial Psychology** lasted longer and then became the current but rather cumbersome term **Industrial and Organizational Psychology** (known as **IO psychology** for short and watch the 'z' in 'organizational'). In this book we will use the terms 'organisational psychology', 'work psychology' or 'occupational psychology' interchangeably to indicate the same area of theory and research.

The confusion of terms partly represents historical development in different societies and partly represents a dissatisfaction with the terms 'industry', 'work' and 'occupational'. Very little remains of the UK industry which existed when industrial psychology first cut its teeth. Many people work in what are now termed 'service industries' and many work in modern technology companies. Many others work in government, education and charitable organisations. Even 'work' in general is not satisfactory since organisations can include those in which most people provide voluntary effort – such as sports clubs, Rotary societies, political parties or self-help groups. 'Work' tends to imply *paid* work whereas the motivations for people to work in voluntary organisation can be very different from those which motivate us in our 'jobs'. Besides, organisational psychology covers a lot more than just the issues concerned with individual occupations and roles.

# Chicken and egg: from application to psychology or from psychology to application?

You will often be told that organisational psychology is the application of theories and research in psychology to the world of work. This is a simplistic and rather misleading notion. In general, many of the most famous and influential theories in psychology have been developed from researchers *already working* in an applied area. One need only think of Freud and Carl Rogers working with neurotic adults, Binet, Burt and Piaget with schoolchildren or Bowlby with young offenders. Social Psychology and the study of Individual Differences, in particular, have been heavily influenced by writers and researchers working *in the field* – that is, not in laboratories but in real work environments trying to solve practical problems of management, motivation and production rather than developing pure psychological theories in academic isolation. For instance, early work on attitude formation and maintenance was developed by American researchers attempting to make World War II troops in the Far East accept that fighting might be long-lasting. The same researchers tried, during that war, to change the attitude of the US public towards the use of offal as acceptable food.

Wartime has been an 'engine of opportunity' (Cox, 2001) for industrial psychology. It has induced several major psychological innovations, for example the first use of mass intelligence testing during WW1 in order to allocate men to appropriate ranks and specialist tasks when there was little time for training. Tests were seen as a scientific way to avoid wastage by matching people to tasks. After the Great War, psychological assessments proliferated for engineers, dress-makers, weavers, box-makers, solderers, machine-operators and the like (Hollway, 1991). Note that these jobs are highly specialised and manual so that evidence of competence is fairly easy to obtain. Tests for predicting good managers or teachers have not been nearly as popular or successful.

Many aspects of social psychology have early roots in the famous **Hawthorne Studies**. These were a long and complex series of research studies beginning in the mid-1920s at the Hawthorne plant of the Western Electric Company in Chicago. Psychologists and other industrial researchers started by experimenting on the effects of varying conditions (e.g. illumination) on the production rates of workers. This highlighted the methodological research problem now well known to psychology students as the 'Hawthorne effect' where behaviour is affected simply through the knowledge that one is being investigated. Workers at the plant appeared to increase production no matter which way the illumination was altered (see Chapter 8). However, Hawthorne gave much more to psychology than just this. Findings from another part of the study emphasised the informal rules, or 'social norms' that develop within small groups and were a foundation for the study of small groups in social psychology, sometimes referred to as **Group Processes**.

In addition, the Hawthorne research work marked a shift in the conception of the worker, and therefore of human beings in general. Under **Taylorism** (see Chapter 7) workers had been seen as rational, machine-like units which produced output (finished goods, machine products etc.) according to instructions. If their production was inadequate this must be the result of misunderstood instructions or 'fatigue'. Indeed, in the UK, the NIIP was preceded by the government funded 'Industrial Fatigue Research Board' which investigated health and other reasons for low performance in workers.

The Hawthorne work resulted in the development of an approach to the management of people known as **Human relations** which dominated the field between the 1930s and 1960s but which is still influential and has become interwoven with new ideas and approaches since then. In some ways this shift mirrors the battle between behaviourism and both cognitive and humanistic approaches within psychology. Basically, Hawthorne had shown that workers had feelings, attitudes, motivation and a need for job satisfaction. In between receiving instructions and the final product of their labours, workers were influenced by relationships in and out of work, by the style of leadership from management, by the meaningfulness of their work, by the organisation of their work groups, by their level of responsibility, by the 'culture' and level of morale of their work place and so on. This is the stuff of this book and the subject matter of organisational psychology.

If you have already studied some psychology you may recognise some of the theories and concepts mentioned above. You'll probably see that they did not just appear at the whim of academics but because of practical work problems which applied scientists were attempting to solve. As a result, organisational psychology has often been the *source* of theories and effects in psychology – not merely the application of existing psychological theories to the world of work. For instance, Hollway (1991) points out that Rensis Likert (most famous to the psychology student for giving us the popular 'Likert scale') was associated with the renowned Hawthorne studies and went on through the 1940s and 1950s to make strong contributions to the study of organisational structures and development. Likert was one of a number of 'great names' associated with Michigan University and with organisational psychology and Human Relations. This list includes Cartwright, Festinger, Deutsch, Lippitt and McGregor.

# Organisational psychology in the UK today

In general, what has organisational psychology achieved and where is it going? Tom Cox (2001) argued that the original 'engines of opportunity' for work psychology were military, especially during the first world war, and that since then, the driving force has been overwhelmingly the finance put into it by organisational management seeking to improve efficiency and, ultimately, profit. Most research has been conducted to help management find ways to motivate and satisfy workers, but with the overriding aim of benefiting the organisation. Since management does the investing, management reaps the rewards – 'he who pays the piper calls the tune'. Not enough of the benefits of organisational psychology, Cox argued, have been passed on to *all* employees. In particular, he felt that the following areas and issues have been neglected and should figure more prominently in work psychology in the coming years:

- the role of the older worker; how to persuade them to stay on at work and how to expose strengths rather than weaknesses
- general health and safety at work (although work stress has become a much researched topic – see chapter 7)
- labour organisations at work
- voluntary organisations.

The rest of this book covers most of the major topics which make up mainstream organisational psychology. However the pace of change in the world of work is itself changing ever more quickly. Most of us are now familiar with the electronic office and are intimately attached to the computer on our desktop. However, research results concerning new technology at work are only slowly filtering into general work psychology textbooks. This book takes a brief look at the impact of e-mail (Chapter 4) but does not have space to look more thoroughly at the ways in which fax, e-mail, mobile phones, laptops, the Internet and intranets have so completely changed the ways we produce and exchange information. Hopefully, by the time you finish your course in organisational psychology there will be more to say on these issues and we will have begun to see some of the developments which Tom Cox anticipated.

## FEATURES OF EACH CHAPTER IN THIS BOOK

Each chapter in this book ends with key terms, exercises and anticipated essay questions, recommended reading and a few useful websites. Here, along with key terms from this introduction are some *general* textbooks for further reading and some websites that may be useful for any topic in organisational psychology.

## KEY TERMS

chartered occupational psychologist
group processes
Hawthorne studies
human relations
industrial and organizational psychology
industrial psychology
IO psychology
occupational psychology
organisational psychology
taylorism
work psychology

# Recommended general reading

Arnold, J., Cooper, C.L. and Robertson, I.T. (1998) *Work Psychology: Understanding human behaviour in the workplace.* London: Financial Times/Pitman Publishing.

Furnham, A. (1997) *The Psychology of Behaviour at Work.* Hove: Psychology Press.

Hollway, W. (1991) *Work Psychology and Organizational Behaviour.* London: Sage.

Miner, J.B. (1992) *Industrial–Organizational Psychology.* New York: McGraw-Hill.

Riggio, R.E. (1999) *Introduction to Industrial and Organizational Psychology (3rd ed)* Upper Saddle River, NJ: Prentice Hall.

# Websites

http://allserv.rug.ac.be/~flievens/op.htm
Occupational psychology survival page – everything! This site also links to many other sites.

http://www.apa.org/journals/
American Psychological Association's site for electronic journals.

http://www.bps.org.uk/
British Psychological Society home page.

http://princess1.bps.org.uk/PUBLICAT/EJOURNALS/op/OP.html
BPS – Journal of Occupational and Organisational Psychology.

http://sosig.esrc.bris.ac.uk/
The Social Science Information Gateway (SOSIG) aims to provide a trusted source of selected, high quality Internet information for researchers and practitioners in the social sciences, business and law. It is part of the UK Resource Discovery Network.

http://www.socialpsychology.org/io.htm
Industrial organisational links in the Social Psychology Network.

# Selection of people for work

# one

## Introduction

The basic goal of selection from the employer's point of view is to select the most effective person for the job. Usually selectors take into account the applicant's likelihood of staying with the organisation and their potential to move into higher level posts, making further contributions to the development and effectiveness of the organisation.

In seeking a person for a job employers typically draw up a job description in terms of the usual tasks required to perform it. This may be achieved through job analysis, a procedure we shall consider in the next chapter. In setting up a selection process employers will then consider what a person needs to demonstrate in order to be considered as the best person for the job. This involves setting out a **person specification** which traditionally includes a list of knowledge, skills and attitudes/abilities (**KSAs**) that would be central to good job performance.

Though the emphasis of selection thinking tends to be on the appointment of new applicants into vacant posts, selection in fact covers a number of procedures for staff changes and organisational development. Figure 1.1 shows some of these major procedures.

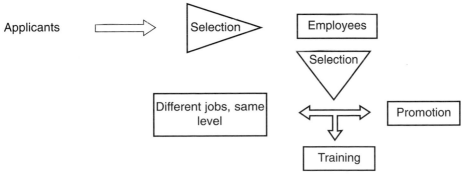

• **Figure 1.1:** Selection procedure

On a sombre note, selection may also be required for redundancy and for early retirement.

In this chapter we shall first consider techniques or 'screening' applicants for posts. In a sense this means passing them through the filter of the person specification to see how well they match up. Psychologists have developed various **psychometric tests** which are instruments which attempt to measure characteristics of people – personality, ability, intelligence and so on. We shall consider the use of these in selection.

We shall then move on to looking at the most common assessment instrument in selection – the face to face interview – and look at possible problems with this procedure. We will end by looking at some of the decisions which selection panels make in finally selecting an applicant for a job. The sections for this chapter then are:

- Personnel selection and psychometric testing
- Types and pitfalls of selection interviews
- Personnel selection decisions.

---

Theme link (**individual differences and job selection**)

One of the earliest applications of psychology to everyday life, and one of the early motivations to extend psychology's practical use, was in the field of personnel selection. The First World War saw the first substantial use of psychological testing. When the United States entered the war in 1917 the US army's Committee for Psychology used the Army Alpha intelligence test to decide on the most appropriate placement for new recruits. Some have cynically viewed this procedure as a method for deciding, in the case of each recruit, whether he be sent to the front as 'canon fodder' or, with marginally better odds for survival, as an officer. Whatever the view, the experience left psychology with a new, positive reputation as a science capable of both helping employers to fit the best worker to the job, but also of helping the worker to find the most fitting job. However, as was suggested in the introduction, **vocational guidance** (helping people find suitable jobs) has benefited from psychological research very little compared with the use that has been made of psychometric testing in personnel selection.

The most optimistic and energetic worker in this field was Sir Cyril Burt, appointed in 1912 by the London County Council as the first ever educational Psychologist in Britain. He promoted the use of psychological tests to measure 'individual differences in mind' (1924, p.67) and he believed wholeheartedly that tests were the instrument for demonstrating innate differences between individuals, sometimes camouflaged by their social standing. He felt that there were bright children living in poverty whose talents were being wasted, whilst there were also many advantaged people who occupied positions unjustified by their actual abilities. The theory of Individual Differences developed hand in hand with the post-war development of psychometric tests. For many years it was believed that humans could be separated mainly on the basis of their innate general intelligence, but also by their position on various subordinate tests of special abilities, such as verbal, numerical and spatial ability and memory.

# Personnel screening and psychometric testing

Personnel screening involves the investigation of information about job applicants' KSAs in order to make a satisfactory appointment. From the selector's point of view, this includes likely productivity, efficiency and tenure (length of stay in the post). If you were selecting someone for the job of psychology lecturer what KSAs might you think important?

## Sample KSAs for a psychology lecturer

| Knowledge | Skills | Attitudes/Abilities |
| --- | --- | --- |
| ➢ Of subject area, thorough and up-to-date | ➢ good communication skills | ➢ conscientious |
| | | ➢ punctual |
| | ➢ ability to teach clearly and with enthusiasm | ➢ warmth towards students |
| ➢ Of educational institutions and administrative procedures | | ➢ belief in the educational system |
| | ➢ administrative efficiency | |
| ➢ Of resources – books, websites, teaching equipment etc. | ➢ information technology competence | ➢ non-discriminatory, non-sexist, non-racist, etc |
| | | ➢ able to exert discipline, fairness, equal treatment etc. |

We need now to consider several ways of assessing what each applicant for the lecturing post can do and how they are likely to perform in future. Below is a list of assessment methods used to 'screen' applicants. Consider which of these might be used to assess the KSAs of each applicant for the lecturing post:

> Review of:
  - CV (curriculum vitae) – includes past teaching experience and achievements
  - Academic qualifications
  - Application form – includes current demographic details (where living at present, current post, salary, responsibilities, reasons for wanting the post
  - Letter of application – also includes current post information but should be tailored specifically to the job description saying why candidate is particularly suited
  - References
> Psychometric test (abilities and personality)
> Face to face interview
> Work sample (performance of actual tasks which are critical to the job)
> Assessment centre (involves a variety of the above procedures).

It may be possible to assess the applicant's state of current knowledge from their letter or CV … But it may not. It all depends upon what the applicant has been asked to do and whether they have provided what has been requested. Certainly, the person's ability to teach will not be clearly evident from the written information, though the selectors might be inclined to believe a glowing report in references.

PSYCHOMETRIC TESTING

Psychometric tests are rarely used in the selection of professionals such as lecturers or doctors. They have been more extensively used where jobs are relatively focused and specific in range, such as lathe operator, clerk, technician or pilot.

Tests tend to fall into one of two major categories, **ability tests** where we are interested in the best people can do, sometimes known as 'maximum performance', and **personality tests** where we are interested in what people are generally like – their *typical* performance.

ABILITY AND APTITUDE TESTS

**Ability tests** measure what a person can do. They are sometimes known as **attainment** or **achievement tests**, thus putting the emphasis on what you have already achieved. **Aptitude tests** are aimed at assessing what you are *potentially* capable of. The term 'aptitude' is often used in the sense of innate (in-born) potential whereas the term 'ability' refers more to what a person has learned to do (see Kline, 1993).

**Psycho-motor tests:** These include, for instance, hand–eye co-ordination tasks and any which include specialised equipment, such as completing a maze or using a driving simulator.

**General ability tests:** These look at broader categories of human psychological functioning such as general intelligence and the so-called 'major group factors' of verbal ability, spatial ability, numerical ability.

**Tests of specific ability:** This is a very broad area of testing and there is a grey area between these and the broader general abilities just mentioned. An example would be the following tests included in the **MOST** (Modern Occupational Skills Tests) battery[1]:

* Verbal checking
* Numerical checking
* Technical checking
* Decision making
* Filing

## PERSONALITY TESTS

Measures of personality and motivation are concerned with what a person is like. Many tests have been developed from 'grand' theories of personality in psychology where researchers have tried to identify and measure relatively stable characteristics of individuals. The Myers-Briggs test, for instance, relies heavily on Jung's psychoanalytic concepts.

**Personality scales** attempt to measure how a person generally is and behaves, their typical approach to life, people, events. Common personality traits or types measured by tests include: anxiety, aggression, extroversion, introversion, self-esteem, aggression, dependency, leadership style and a whole range of attitudes.

**Personal interest inventories** measure a person's interests in life, in particular their interest in different types of occupation, their orientation towards people or things and so on. They would be of particular use in careers and occupational guidance, or in guidance for training and personal development.

**Motivation scales** concern people's drive and desire especially in the world of work and their chosen job. Examples would be measures of 'Need for Achievement' and 'Job Satisfaction'.

Since there is a great deal of conflict between the various theoretical models of human personality, the use of personality tests in personnel selection can

1 The Modern Occupational Skills Test battery, Windsor: ASE

be controversial. It would be highly discriminatory to use measures on a theoretical concept, such as 'extroversion' or 'dependency' for which there is nowhere near universal agreement, in order to bar one person from a job and accept another. By contrast, the use of ability tests is far less controversial because they generally possess greater *validity* and *reliability* – see below. Agreement on the validity of personality tests (what they actually measure) is much harder to achieve than for ability tests.

Employers however tend to be more interested in personality than in ability. Bartram *et al* (1995) surveyed some 498 small UK businesses and found that selectors placed far more emphasis on the applicants' personality (e.g. honesty, integrity) and interest in the job than they did on ability, aptitude and attainment.

## BENEFITS, USEFULNESS AND LIMITATIONS OF TESTS

In a traditional job interview, as we shall see below, there is wide scope for bias because people are fickle. Even seasoned interviewers cannot help being swayed at times by the general appearance and social skills of a candidate, even when these characteristics do not form part of the criteria for the job. For instance, a welder should be chosen because he or she can weld very well, not because they are physically attractive or can speak very nicely. Of course, we may also be interested in their ability to work as part of a team or their tendency to absenteeism, but these qualities are not necessarily easily assessed in a face to face interview. Where there is a potential for personal bias in selection the use of tests can:

- Improve the fairness of the selection procedure
- Improve the means for providing equality of opportunity
- Increase productivity by selecting the most efficient employees
- Lower costs of training by selecting those who are better suited to the job
- Lower costs of recruitment by selecting those who are more likely to enjoy the job and stay in it
- Improve relations among the workforce as a result of an impression of fair selection methods
- Increase efficiency through effective deployment of staff.

## limitations of psychometric tests in selection

The fact that tests discriminate is not a problem but should be a strength. After all, what we want them to do is to discriminate fairly between potentially good and weaker employees, in the sense that the 'good' ones are best suited to the job. However, where tests discriminate unfairly against *groups* or *categories* of people the problem can be legal as well as moral. Psychometric tests may unintentionally discriminate unfairly against certain groups. General intelligence tests have often been found to favour those with superior language skills and where good verbal skill is not a requirement for good job performance this would be a discriminatory test. Although the debate about the effect of cultural factors on various psychological tests is extremely broad and often very heated, it is highly likely that some tests will discriminate unfairly against members of certain minority ethnic groups. This was certainly true in the early days of testing when general intelligence tests in the USA, used to screen newly arrived immigrants, included questions about sports stars and characters in advertisements. The general language used in tests is likely to be more familiar to some than to others, in terms of ethnicity and social class. Having said this, tests are scored, once taken, with no reference to the respondent's gender, culture or class. In a face to face interview, as we shall see, there is far more scope for these factors to influence the panel's decision.

In order to be measures that we can trust, psychological tests need to be both reliable and valid. Reliability refers to the test being *consistent* while validity refers to the test measuring what it is supposed to measure. Ability tests do better on these criteria than do personality tests but no test is perfect.

Psychological test results alone will not give an employer a rounded picture of the person they are proposing to employ, why that person really wants the job, their history of absenteeism, their punctuality and ability to keep to deadlines. Most important of all they will not tell the selector what the person is like face to face and they will not provide information on how the person actually performs on a task.

Employers use a number of procedures for selecting new staff **Section summary** from the applicant pool. Their aim is to select the most effective person for the job. Selection requires thorough prior knowledge of the job and of the person's experience and abilities. Psychological tests have advantages over the interview in terms of reducing personal bias and prejudice and concentrating on specific skills. However they can be discriminatory, they are often weak on reliability and validity and they do not present a picture of the whole person.

# The selection interview

You have probably undergone some sort of interview process in your life, if only as a prelude to entering a certain school or for a part-time job. Many interviews appear to be just a kind of informal chat where the interviewer gets to see how you talk, how alert you are perhaps, and just what you look like. Usually no aspect of the job itself is directly tested. Not being psychologists, most informal interviewers are highly likely to fall back on personal experience, prejudice, untrustworthy first impressions and stereotyped expectations. What is most likely to happen is that, of all the people who fit the person specification, the one selected will be the one who is liked, the most physically attractive or the one who 'just seems to fit', rather than the person who is actually best for the job. In some cases personality and looks are requirements for the job, but very often they are not, yet these may well be the hidden criteria for selection. For these reasons probably, the interview has often been found to be relatively ineffective as the only tool in a selection process, for example by Hunter and Hunter, 1984. However, the *structured interview* (see below), in which selectors may only ask job-related questions and must follow a specified order of questioning, has been shown to produce superior results as measured by, for instance, the later performance and tenure of successful applicants (Huffcut and Arthur, 1994).

Gender and ethnic origin are likely to be biasing factors. In a study of real job interviewers Graves and Powell (1996) showed, surprisingly and in contrast to earlier work, that female interviewers rated female candidates' performance higher than males' whereas male interviewers showed no gender bias. A 1985 Commission for Racial Equality study showed that minority ethnic group members were significantly less successful in being selected for employment in Leicester despite having similar qualifications and experience. Brown and Gay (1985) found that Asian applicants matched on gender, experience and qualifications were far less successful in even being called for interview. A recent simulation study (Awosunle and Doyle, 2001), though conducted in a laboratory, showed that, on the basis of accent alone, black candidates were rated as more suitable for a job by black selectors whereas whites were seen as more suitable by whites.

If the selection interview is going to be fair and effective it needs to be seen for what it is: another tool of human measurement. However it is likely that many interviewers do not see the interview this way. Below is a list of pitfalls in interviewing that can contribute to making this process one of the most unfair, subjective and ineffective methods of selecting personnel:

➤ Interview questions not standard and likelihood of 'drifting' during any one session, therefore not covering essential areas which are covered for other applicants.

➤ Questions unfair as not all related to the job and some find these easier than others (e.g. 'Tell us about your hobbies').

➤ Interviewers in a panel do not assess on identical characteristics but just have a free-for-all discussion after all have been seen. Hence comparisons are arbitrary.

➤ Untrained interviewers, and those with serious prejudices, may base their decision on dislike of the person (or their category) rather than on job-related criteria.

Riggio (1990) provides several criteria which, research shows, will improve the validity and reliability of the selections made:

**Structured interview:** If the same basic questions are asked of all applicants, not only is this fair but it also carries two distinct advantages. First, comparisons can be made and second, the interview stays on a planned course and questions do not wander.

**Questions job related:** Questions can be developed following a thorough job analysis. In particular, Latham and Saari (1984) have shown greater job success prediction using a *situational interview* in which questions are based on critical incidents and applicants describe how they would respond in certain critical conditions (e.g. when a customer complains, when one team member is off sick).

**Use a scoring system:** Good structured interviews ask interviewers to rate each candidate on several criteria directly after the interviews. Particularly effective are systems where interviewers agree beforehand what would count as an adequate or a very good response.

**Interviewer training:** Interviewers can be trained to avoid systematic bias in their judgements about people, especially stereotyped assumptions about gender, ethnicity, disability, sexual preference and so on. They can also be trained to interview in a fair and relaxed manner which obtains the best from each candidate and does not intimidate them.

**Panels:** The advantages of a *panel* of interviewers is that extreme views and biased judgements might be spotted and counterbalanced by alternative points of view. The disadvantages are time and cost. In addition, a panel may all labour under the same stereotyped misinterpretations of behaviour, in which case the victim of such judgements has even less chance of being selected.

**Efficient use of interview time:** A structured interview can avoid unnecessary questions which simply repeat information which is already available elsewhere, for instance on the application form.

As Riggio reports, Campion, Pursell and Brown (1988) showed that an interview process employing many of the above features produced high reliability and good prediction of future job performance in a paper mill.

> **Section summary**
>
> The traditional interview often does not assess specific skills required for the job and can be affected by irrelevant inter-personal variables such as looks and manner. Structured (e.g. situational) interviews where panel members are trained, questions are pre-set and a standardised scoring (rating) system is employed can be much fairer and more efficient selection tools.

# Personnel selection decisions

Employers usually have to bear in mind the costs and benefits of personnel selection. Traditionally the selection method of choice has been the interview with interviewers using speculation, common sense and practical experience to decide who will make a good worker. Very rarely do small employers make a more scientific attempt to check up on their hunches by measuring predictors and following through to see whether people high on the predictors actually do turn out to be more effective or productive workers. Large organisations cannot just trust their intuitions and must seek to make savings by generally selecting the more efficient worker. They can do this because they have a larger body of empirical data on which to draw. That is, they can keep records of what characteristics in applicants were associated with subsequent high levels of efficiency. They have large samples so they are able to make more scientifically accurate predictions – see Figure 1.2.

• **Figure 1.2:** If scores on logical ability correlate with later performance as an electrician, selectors have a useful predictor

## SELECTION RATIOS

A **selection ratio** is simply the ratio of jobs to applicants and is given as the fraction jobs/applicants. Where there are 10 jobs for 100 applicants the ratio is 0.1. Where the ratio is greater than 1 then the use of selection methods is of little benefit as the employer has to take anyone who applies with the minimum qualifications for the job. Where the ratio is low however, it makes financial sense to employ a selection method which should in principle pick out those most likely to be efficient workers. There are several methods for achieving this.

## CUT-OFF CRITERIA

Suppose it was shown that the better an applicant's dexterity test score the better they perform a certain machine operating job. Although this is a rather simplified example we can see that it makes sense to select those applicants who score highest on this test, all other things being equal. Hence a selection panel might set a cut-off point score on the test so that only applicants scoring higher than this score are selected.

The cut-off point could form part of a *multi-stage* selection procedure whereby applicants successful on the test pass through to the next selection stage: another test, an interview or, better still, a work sample. Some selection procedures might employ a **multiple cut-off point** procedure in which it is necessary for applicants to equal or exceed several cut-off points on several selection variables in order to be considered for employment.

Finally, selection might involve the use of **multiple regression**. This is a statistical technique that relies upon the concept of *correlation*. Earlier we noted that a predictor is good if high scores on it are related to later high scores on job performance. Such a relationship, where scores on one variable are closely related to scores on another, is known as a correlation. Where we use scores on one variable to *predict* scores on a second variable we talk of *regression*. Multiple regression is a technique that, in a way, selects the best *combination* of correlations between predictors and performance so that one may *compensate* for another – see Figure 1.3. In this system, being rather weak on one predictor may be balanced out by being particularly strong on another. However, this will not always work and the selectors may have to include some minimal requirements, similar to cut-off points. For instance, selectors for teaching posts might decide that no matter how good an applicant is on their specialised subject, if they are poor communicators they will be ineffective in the post offered.

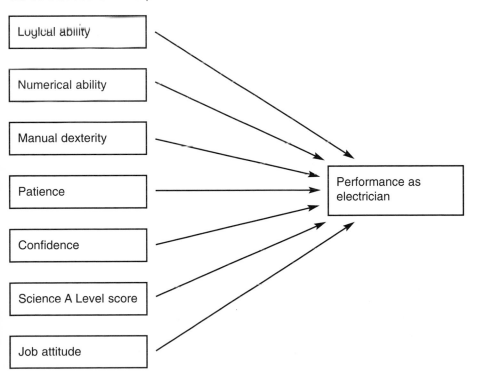

• **Figure 1.3:** If several predictors correlate with performance then selectors can use multiple regression to combine predictors and obtain the best possible estimate of future job performance

FINANCIAL UTILITY OF PSYCHOLOGICAL TESTS

There are several obvious advantages to the use of psychological tests but many employers like to be given clear evidence of financial benefit before changing their ways. Several researchers (especially Schmidt, Mack and Hunter, 1984) have argued that if organisations were to include psychological tests in their selection procedures the costs of doing this would be easily outweighed by the economic benefits. Where the selection ratio is low it pays to cut through the errors involved in selecting people with biased procedures (such as the interview where personality, presentation and looks may distract selectors from assessing the exact skills required for the job). The **utility analysis** approach argues that by using tests which are known to predict later performance in job-related tasks, those who are more likely to make a success of the job will be selected, in theory at least. More successful personnel are also more likely to stay and to contribute positively to the organisation. This approach calculates the financial savings made by using tests as against not using them.

Bartram and Lindley (1994) reviewed research evidence, some of which supports the theoretical predictions of utility analysis. They found, among other things, that:

- ability and aptitude tests tend to be the best single predictors of training performance and job success, though prediction is improved somewhat by their combination with other forms of assessment
- ability and aptitude tests predict job success better than educational level, interviewer judgement and previous employers' reports, though equally effective prediction can be obtained using work sample tests
- batteries of (i.e. several) ability tests predict performance better than an individual test.

**Section summary**    Selectors must eventually base their decisions on some form of objectively measurable criteria. These are often cut-off points on previously agreed scales and tests. The lower is the selection ratio the more the organisation can benefit from effective selection decisions. Utility analysis argues that use of psychological tests will create financial savings in the long run over large numbers. Research has suggested which combinations of tests will predict job success.

## KEY TERMS

ability tests
aptitude tests
attainment or achievement tests
cut-off criteria
general ability tests
(KSAs)
motivation scales
multiple cut-off points
multiple regression
personal interest inventories
personality tests
personnel screening
person specification
psychometric tests
psycho-motor tests
selection interview
selection ratio
situational interview
structured interview
tests of specific ability
utility analysis
vocational guidance

## EXERCISE 1

Draw up a table of KSAs that you think might be required for the
jobs of:

- Nursery nurse
- Police officer
- High-speed train driver

Compare your answers with colleagues and come to a joint
decision on what might appear in a person specification for these
jobs.

**EXERCISE 2**

Draw up a table of characteristics (e.g. hair length, accent) which
might affect interview selectors but which usually are not
specifically relevant to how well a job will be performed. Now, for
each of these characteristics, try to think of jobs where that
characteristic might be an essential item of the person specification
(for instance, does Santa Claus have to be male?).

**ESSAY QUESTIONS**

1. Critically evaluate the use of psychological tests in the selection
   of applicants for jobs.

2. Discuss ways in which job interviews can be made more fair
   and more effective.

3. Critically assess the decisions that selection panels must make
   in choosing appropriate applicants for jobs.

# Further reading

Arnold, J.S.A., Cooper, C.L. and Robertson, I.T. (1998) *Work Psychology:
   Understanding Human behaviour in the workplace*. London: Financial
   Times Pitman. Chapters 7 and 8.
Smith, J.M. and Robertson, I.T. (1993) *The Theory and Practice of Systematic
   Personnel Selection*. London: Macmilllan.

# Websites

http://bized.ac.uk/fme/3i.htm# (Bized's site on selection)

http://www.ipd.co.uk/ Institute of Personnel and Development

# two

# Human resource practices

## Introduction

In order to make fair job appointments and have it clearly understood what a specific job entails there is a need for thorough and accurate job analysis – an objective summary of a job's requirements and limits. It is no good telling someone that they haven't done their job properly if they don't exactly know what that entails. It is likely to cause great resentment if one employee is rewarded while another who happens to be doing much more in their job, is not. This chapter looks first at the concept and techniques of job analysis and then at the ways in which we can assess the extent to which employees are satisfactorily meeting their job requirements – **performance appraisal**. Finally we look at the kinds of reward systems that often depend upon good analysis and appraisal. This last topic is intimately connected with the topics of work motivation and job satisfaction which we will return to in Chapters 6 and 7. The sections for this chapter then are:

- **Job analysis and job analysis techniques**
- **Performance appraisal, techniques, administration and problems**
- **Reward systems.**

## Job analysis techniques

Some time ago a fire service in California used to include in its criteria for selection as a fire-fighter the requirement that applicants carry a 200lb weight over an obstacle course. Very few women were successful and hence few were appointed. The criterion was challenged and a job analysis carried out. This showed that the carrying task was rarely if ever required in order to perform the job of fire-fighter satisfactorily. The criterion was ruled discriminatory and removed from the selection procedure.

The problem here was that the person specification did not match the job description. The purpose of a job analysis is to produce a job description, in terms of skills, abilities, knowledge and equipment, by studying the work of several people who do that job. The results might be used for:

- *Developing a valid selection procedure* – by producing a job description and person specification in order to match applicants against job requirements. Wiesner and Cronshaw (1988) showed that job selection interviews based on job analysis were superior in outcome to those that were not.
- *Job evaluation* – one of the most important uses. Job evaluation involves comparing one job with another in some quantitative manner so that wages and benefits (e.g. car) appropriate to jobs can be decided upon. Note that this is done for jobs, not persons who currently happen to hold that job.
- *Specifying training needs* – personnel might need training so that they are competent in all aspects of the job.
- *Job redesign* – where changes are made so that jobs are more interesting, safer or more suitably geared to human abilities and needs.
- *Reducing ambiguity* – very often there is a discrepancy between what workers say they do and what the organisation says they should do.

## JOB ANALYSIS TECHNIQUES

In order to gather data on the actual content of specific jobs, organisational psychologists employ several familiar research techniques.

### observation

Direct observation of a worker's activities has the advantage of highlighting behaviour or tasks which the interview might not, simply because workers fail to mention them or consider them unimportant. This can work effectively for simple repetitive and manual tasks. However problems would be encountered where:

- The job involves mainly mental activity which cannot be observed (e.g. writing a lecture).
- Job-holders are aware of the observation: the worker might be subject to the 'Hawthorne effect' (see p.117) where knowledge of observation itself seriously affects the way the observed person behaves.
- The job or task cycle is long: farming tasks can involve both planting and reaping; writing new software might take several months or even years.

## interview

The problems above are mostly answered by the interview method, but this brings problems of its own. The advantages are that job-holders have information about their jobs that may not be available by any other method. They can be active in the analysis process and so may be less alienated by the attention their job is receiving. However possible dangers include:

- Interviewees might anticipate rewards or redundancies based on the information they provide and hence may distort the nature and importance of the job accordingly.
- Lack of rapport between interviewer and jobholder because the wrong level of terminology is used (e.g. overly formal), the jobholder distrusts the interviewer or has been inadequately prepared for the process.
- A poorly prepared set of questions. Asking people just to 'tell me about your job' will not produce consistent information. Interview questions need to be prepared with a closer relationship to the precise information required from the job analysis.

Interviews would normally be conducted with several job holders and/or with supervisors and subordinates in order to 'triangulate' information (use several perspectives) to get an overall picture.

## the questionnaire or task inventory

This method is often called a *self-report* approach since employees usually tick off or give a rating to each item on the questionnaire. Typically this will consist of very many task statements (such as 'lubricate bearings' or 'make telephone calls') which the employee simply ticks (as being part of the job) or rates on a numbered scale which indicates 'how important' or 'how frequently' the task is performed. The task statements are generated through consultation with job experts prior to scale construction.

## SPECIFIC METHODS OF JOB ANALYSIS

**Functional Job Analysis** (FJA), unlike task inventories which relate only to specific jobs, can be used to compare very different jobs (see Fine, 1988). It takes a large list of tasks, already generated from the study of a job, and grades these according to the categories shown in Table 2.1. Eventually the job itself is given an overall grading according to its 'orientation'. This refers to the relative degree to which the job is involved in three major areas – data, people and things. FJA is useful in comparing jobs for equivalence (in terms of salary etc.) and in producing job descriptions where large numbers of positions are involved.

• **Table 2.1:** Areas and levels used in Functional Job Analysis

| Data | People | Things |
|------|--------|--------|
| 0. Synthesising<br>1. Co-ordinating<br>2. Analysing<br>3. Compiling<br>4. Computing<br>5. Copying<br>6. Comparing | 0. Mentoring<br>1. Negotiating<br>2. Instructing<br>3. Supervising<br>4. Diverting<br>5. Persuading<br>6. Speaking–signalling.<br>7. Serving<br>8. Taking instructions–<br>   helping | 0. Setting up<br>1. Precision working<br>2. Operating–controlling<br>3. Driving–operating<br>4. Manipulating<br>5. Tending<br>6. Feeding–offbearing<br>7. Handling |

The **Position Analysis Questionnaire** (PAQ) developed by McCormick, Jeaneret and Mecham (1972) also permits comparison across different jobs. It is more detailed than the FJA and consists of nearly 200 items under each of six major headings: information input (e.g. reading dials, inspection), mediation (mental processes), work output (e.g. equipment, physical co-ordination), relationships with other persons (e.g. communication), job context (e.g. dealing with conflict) and other job characteristics (a catch-all category). Originally the scale required the reading ability of a college graduate (Ash and Edgell, 1975). Revisions have been made but the reading level required is still quite high.

British scales have been produced following on the success of the PAQ. Banks *et al.*, 1983, developed the **Job Components Inventory** (JCI) which produces a measure of the skills required for a job. Saville and Holdsworth's **Work Profiling System** (SHL, 1988, updated in 1995) uses over 800 items of which 200 are used for any particular job.

**Critical incidents technique** (Flanagan, 1954) involves asking job-holders or supervisors for examples of very good or very poor performance. For instance, workers might be asked to recall the last job that they feel they did really well. These incidents are recorded along with the specific behaviour patterns and events that were associated with the incident. A problem with this technique is that while it might identify particularly useful behaviours and those to be avoided, it might not identify the typical but unremarkable aspects of a job. In addition, it is found that respondents tend to attribute incidents to personality rather than to actual behaviour, saying 'he was clumsy' rather than 'he found difficulty in operating this lever here', see Theme Link 2.

Section summary

A job analysis is required before one can draw up a job description in order to interview fairly for new posts. Job analyses are crucial if fairness and objectivity are going to occur in selection, promotion, training, job evaluation, performance awards and so on. They are also necessary before an attempt is made to redesign jobs. Several techniques have been discussed and the appropriateness, advantages and weaknesses of these depend on the purposes of the analysis and the specific work context.

# Performance appraisal

Once we have identified through job analysis what a particular job entails, it makes sense to see whether a job-holder is in fact doing that job effectively. Because this process of **performance appraisal** may affect pay awards and promotion, employers must assess workers' efforts in a consistent and formal manner. Traditionally appraisal was conducted informally by untrained supervisors and so suffered from superficial impressions, prejudice and hearsay. Because this approach was not objective, organisations started to use formal appraisal systems to assess more accurately how well each employee was meeting targets.

### WHY APPRAISE EMPLOYEES?

Before reading on try to think now of several advantages, psychologically speaking, of appraising employees' performance.

- Feedback – cognitive theories in psychology tell us that people require feedback on their performance for two very good reasons. First, this allows them to know how well they are doing. A long history of the study of the effects of 'knowledge of results' on performance shows that such knowledge helps people perform better in future. Second, feedback also motivates people by letting them know where they stand in the system.
- Rewards – appraisal can also be seen as a fair way of distributing rewards, bonuses and promotions. It is better to compare people openly, through a formal system, than to leave people feeling that they might do well so long as they get to know and please the right people.
- Training and development – identification of each employee's future training needs should be a direct and useful outcome of a good appraisal system. This is another motivating factor for the employee as they have their needs recognised and can strive after better positions. It is also useful for the organisation in ensuring that it builds up a desirable set of competencies among staff. Further, the process can help identify potential among staff – those employees ready for further challenges.

However, from the worker's point of view, performance appraisal has often been met with suspicion and hostility. Understandably trades unions have seen the process as a threat to members' jobs. Managers, too, often fear they cannot be fair to workers with whom they do not interact on a day to day level. In addition they can see the process as confrontational and likely to nurture dislike and distrust among their workers. Roberts (1994) found that acceptance of appraisal systems depended upon two major factors:

**Employee voice:** The extent to which employees could participate in discussion at their appraisal, negotiate the goals to be set *with* the appraiser/manager; the extent to which employees could discuss the feedback on their performance without fear of sanction.

**Information validity:** The extent to which employees perceived truthfulness in the content of appraisals; the employee's acceptance that the appraisal process had some effect on decisions made in the organisation, it wasn't just all 'hot air'; the extent to which employees could see the justification for the targets they were set, could understand these goals and could see how to attain them, i.e. not impossible targets.

Put simply, you are more likely to accept appraisal when you can discuss openly your boss's view of your performance, when you agree goals with your boss and are not just told what to do, where you can see how to do the things you have agreed to do, where your task does not seem impossible and where you know when to do things by. If you can also see that the results of your appraisal are important in deciding how your department moves forward then you are more likely to accept your appraisal experience and see it as valid.

MEASURING PERFORMANCE

Measurement of performance must rely fairly directly upon the results of the job analysis process discussed in the last section. If we know the job criteria then we should be able to measure up performance against these. How might you assess performance in the job of:

- McDonald's service assistant
- College lecturer or teacher?

In the McDonald's post we might measure speed of service, number of orders or money-taking errors, number of customer complaints. The job of teacher is far harder to assess. Of course one measure might be examination passes, but most people accept that a high number of passes is not the sole target of teaching. There is a quality in teaching that is hard to assess. How do we measure a target of 'generating enthusiasm'? Perhaps by the number of students leaving the class early, or student evaluations, but these are indirect measures of actual teaching success.

## rating scales

For the assessment of relatively simple performances, rating scales have been very popular. A McDonald's observer might give a score from 1 (poor) to 5 (excellent) on any of the following as examples: responsiveness to waiting customers, accuracy in completing orders, operation of machinery and politeness.

The use of a scale to assess behaviour involves several problems. First, how are we to know that one observer will rate the same way as another? This is the issue of reliability, as discussed in the Theme Link below.

Theme link 1 (**Methodology**)

**Reliability and validity.** Psychological measures need to be reliable. This has to do with consistency. If you use a tyre pressure gauge you want to be sure that a reading of 30 psi measures the same amount on Monday as it does on Tuesday. You can cope with the gauge being 5 psi out just so long as it always gives a consistent measure for the same quantity. This is also the case for psychological and performance measures. A measure of creative thinking should produce, by and large, the same score on one occasion as it does on another for each individual tested. We also want a measure of competence, based on human observation, to be reliable. In the context of appraisal, there are two important ways in which we should expect observer or rater reliability:

**Intra-rater:** we expect the same rater to give the same score for the same level observed on any occasion.
**Inter-rater:** we expect two different raters to give the same score for the same behaviour.

In both these situations we can use correlation between pairs of scores. For intra-rater reliability we could ask the same observer to rate many (recorded) examples, several of which are repeated. We would correlate the pairs of scores on these repeated instances. The observer should give much the same score on each occasion. For inter-rater reliability we would obtain the two observers' scores on several instances and simply correlate these pairs.

Ideally we would also like our scales to be valid – that is, they measure what they are intended to measure. It may be the case that 'politeness' really only measures an assistant's ability to repeat automatically stock phrases like 'have a nice day'. Assuming that a competence measure does validly cover the intended behaviour, we need to train our observers in the meaning of the measure, then use a lot of practice with feedback in order to increase reliability and ensure validity.

A further possible problem with rating scales is what is known as the **halo effect**. This is the tendency to see a person as good (or bad) on all measures because they are particularly good (or bad) on one central measure. A punctual, tidy person may also be seen as efficient and productive, when in fact they are only average on these last two characteristics. Fletcher (1995) found that sets of such attributes were correlated far more than they should have been and raters seemed to be particularly influenced by conscientiousness and optimism. Staff high on these characteristics were also rated highly on quite unrelated characteristics such as 'quality of judgement'.

## objective measures

These include performance outcomes such as number of houses sold, number of burgers produced and even include measuring teachers by their pupil pass rate.

## job samples

Other methods of assessment include testing job knowledge and job sample proficiency. An appraiser might observe short simulations of the job such as laying a restaurant place or taking a booking.

## development dialogues

An alternative to traditional assessment of behaviour in a performance appraisal session was advocated in 1993 by Larsen and Bang. Although originating in Scandinavian countries, this system is familiar to many working in the UK educational system. The idea is to sit down on an equal basis and discuss the employee's present motivation, job performance and responsibilities. These are reviewed in the light of previously agreed job targets and objectives. Then new objectives are agreed (not simply set by the appraiser) along with a discussion of what the employee likes and dislikes about their present job, barriers they face, career prospects and consequent training needs to meet objectives and develop their career.

## who conducts the performance appraisal?

The person who conducts formal appraisal of workers' performances is almost always the line manager – that is, the person who directly manages the worker. However, as customers, we all contribute indirectly towards appraisal of service staff when we fill in those little questionnaires: 'Was your car tidy when you collected it? Had it been washed and vacuumed satisfactorily?', or when we answer a post-sales customer care telephone enquiry. You may well have been asked to evaluate your tutor's performance on quite a number of dimensions. If not, ask why not!

Theme link 2 (**Social psychology and attribution theory**)

Attribution theory tells us that people in general, at least in the West, have a particular bias when interpreting the causes of people's behaviour. We can make an *internal* or an *external* attribution. If we see a person's behaviour as caused mainly by the way that a person is, by their intentions or their permanent character (e.g. 'I'm not surprised, he's a very mean person'; 'she is so clumsy') then we are making an **internal attribution.** If however we see the external environment as the major cause of an action (e.g. he couldn't afford it; he'd just been though an expensive divorce; she couldn't have known the council had dug up the road) then we make an **external attribution.** Western studies have shown that people are usually far more ready to make internal than external attributions – we tend to blame the person more than the situation they were in. This applies to appraisers as much as to anyone else.

## PROBLEMS IN APPRAISAL

We have seen above that employees tend to be wary of appraisal, and some managers too. Theme link 1 shows us that the measures used to assess performance are subject to various sources of error, as are any attempts to measure human behaviour and there are many known biases involved in human assessment of other human behaviour. Theme link 2 demonstrates that appraisers will need training in the assessment of human behaviour if they are to avoid making very common errors of judgement when assessing the sources of their subordinates' mistakes and successes.

One way to avoid the errors involved in a single appraiser's view of an employee is the recent innovation of '360 degree feedback', particularly used in the assessment of managers and supervisors. In this system an employee is rated by peers, subordinates, line manager, clients and so on. It also includes a self-assessment (see Lewthwaite-Patel, 2001, for a case study). The idea is that the appraisee receives views from all angles. For managers the process is particularly powerful since traditionally managers are appraised only by their own superiors not by their staff. An exercise at W.H.Smith's (reported in Chmiel, 2000) resulted in managers hearing that, though they were scoring well on decision-making, they were not seen as good listeners, motivators or developers of their staff. The appraisal process stimulated a newly designed training and development programme for managers.

**Section summary**    Performance appraisal is the assessment of an employee's success in meeting agreed goals. Very often, rewards are dependent upon a satisfactory outcome. The process needs to be treated sensitively and measures must be objective and fair. Various data gathering techniques are discussed and several specific types of process are described. Problems with appraisal can occur if measures are not appropriate or are poorly implemented. Problems occur where employees are not actively involved in the process and are suspicious of the purpose of the assessment process. Supervisors too can be wary of the possible confrontation and unpleasantness involved. Appraisers need training in the observation and interpretation of human performance, particularly to avoid attribution biasing effects.

# Reward systems

One purpose of appraisal is to set future goals and targets. Though we will discuss motivation in general in Chapter 6, clearly people will not work towards goals unless they are motivated. Motivation can be intrinsic or extrinsic. **Intrinsic motivation** is internal to us. Our reward is the sheer challenge and enjoyment of the task and the satisfaction of seeing it through. People can be intrinsically motivated to climb mountains or to spend hours every day building their own kitchen extension. However, no matter how much intrinsic motivation a job may offer us we nevertheless always expect some **extrinsic motivation** from employment. That is we expect external rewards, mostly pay, but also sickness and pension benefits, perhaps a car, expenses and bonuses. Appraisal is closely linked to the topic of motivation in the sense that the future goals which are set may well not be achieved without adequate incentive offered by the organisation.

Rewards and punishments figure strongly in the **behaviourist** model of human behaviour – see Theme link 3. To behaviourists motivation is an explanatory concept we use to explain increases in performance, but we never actually observe it. Behaviourists therefore define motivation only in terms of what is measurable. What we see and can measure is simply the relationship between rewards and work performance. We offer more money or bigger cars and performance rate goes up. Of course the explanatory model of behaviourism is too crude but it does emphasise a couple of important factors in the world of work. First, rewards work far more effectively than punishments (also a useful principle in teaching and child care!) and second, rewards can come in a variety of shapes and sizes, depending upon what is reinforcing for a particular individual.

## Theme link 3 (**Behaviourism and reinforcement**)

The behaviourist model of operant conditioning argues that all we need to understand why people produce behaviour ('responses') is a scientifically accurate record of what stimuli preceded the response and the nature of any direct consequence of it – often called a 'reinforcement'. Rather than defining reinforcement in terms of what actually strengthens our behaviour (e.g. a reward of food or money) Skinner (1953) produced a rather circular explanation that responses were strengthened by reinforcement and that reinforcement was anything that strengthened a response by following it. Positive reinforcement includes anything that increases performance because we *receive* it and negative reinforcement is anything that improves performance because it is *removed* from us – for example, we would be more likely to do a particular exercise if it resulted in decreasing back pain. Note that negative reinforcement is not punishment, although many writers do confuse these terms. Punishment is an attempt to weaken, not strengthen, behaviour by following a response with something aversive, for example, being cross with someone who swears in the hope of inhibiting the bad language. Notably, the major findings of conditioning theories have resulted from experiments with animals and are only sometimes reconfirmed in humans.

Taylorism (see Chapter 7) emerged at about the same time as early behaviourism and was very much in tune with it. Taylorism stated that if jobs could be reduced to very simple repetitive behaviours then it would be relatively simple to record the rate of work and any fluctuations in it due to incentives or sanctions. This principle was indeed a central aspect of scientific management.

## CONDITIONING IS NOT ENOUGH – WORKERS THINK TOO!

However, in practice it is very difficult to view the reward system in an organisation as comparable with conditioning experiments for various reasons. Perhaps the most obvious reason is that major rewards do not always appear immediately *after* appropriate behaviour has been performed, as in animal conditioning experiments. In humans, cognitive processes are necessary to link behaviour with later rewards. Most people are given a monetary reward at most once a week. I never see any money at all associated with work since my salary is paid into a bank account once a month.

Konke and Wright-Isak, 1982, saw the reward system in an organisation as an **inducements–contributions balance**. This is a more cognitive model which sees the employees as weighing the factors which induce them to work (money, intrinsic satisfaction with the work, social contact, benefits) against the contribution they are willing to make. Companies need to offer salaries and benefits that are competitive with other organisations yet keep a balance within their own organisation in order to avoid conflict, jealousy and subsequent dissatisfaction. This often breaks down when one particular type of employee is hard to attract and is paid far higher than comparable people in other jobs. There have been many spectacular examples of this in recent years within British industry where executives receive fantastic multi-million pound salaries on the argument that this is what it takes to attract the best. This wouldn't seem so dubious if it weren't for the fact that in many instances, bonuses and share options in the millions have been awarded even in the face of the company's blatant failure to produce good services or profits.

With more modestly paid jobs, the organisation needs to conduct a job analysis, follow this with job evaluation, then attach rewards as objectively as possible, bearing in mind the skills, knowledge and abilities required in each position.

## INCENTIVE SYSTEMS — GROUPS, CO-OPERATION AND INDIVIDUAL COMPETITION

Salary and benefits are often not very flexible or dynamic motivators. Many companies operate **incentive systems** in order to increase motivation. Miner (1992) discusses two types of system, **merit-pay** and **bonus**. Merit-pay systems award wage increases to better performers, whereas bonus systems award a single cash sum when performance is rated as good. In fact rewards can be **co-operative**, where the group is rewarded for success, **individualistic**, based on individual performance irrespective of others, or **competitive**, where one person receiving a reward entails that others do not, basically a prize system.

The UK is an individualistically oriented culture, meaning that it tends to praise individual freedom and enterprise. Our level of **collectivism** is relatively low (see Triandis, 1994). Unlike countries like Korea or Japan, we tend to think more in terms of the individual competing for excellence than in terms of our group (family, work team, school group) succeeding. Given this cultural orientation in the UK, it has been quite usual for managers to assume that they can get the best out of workers by offering competitive rewards, that is, by setting worker against worker. Research however has shown that this kind of reward system fails when co-operation is required in a task. If each worker is thinking about doing their best in order to receive a reward, they are hardly likely to act co-operatively, share information or help others to succeed.

Students may sympathise with the work of Deutsch (1949) who formed students into two groups. Co-operative groups, where all individuals in the group received, as their assignment mark, the group grade for the work produced, and competitive groups where each individual was graded according to how well they had contributed towards the group product. The groups rewarded on a co-operative basis tended to produce more in quality and in quantity than the competitive groups. Many studies have confirmed the finding that rewarding people as a group for co-operative work has greater benefits than individual, competitive rewards. Johnson *et al.* (1981) conducted a meta-analytic review of 122 studies with 286 findings and claimed that, in promoting achievement and productivity:

- Co-operation is more effective than individual competition or lone effort.
- Co-operation in groups with competition between groups is similarly superior.
- There is no significant difference between individual competition or lone effort.

## INCENTIVES AND HIGHER HUMAN NEEDS

Kranzusch (1997) argues from employer and employee interviews that simple reward systems ignore higher human motivational needs. He relates these to Maslow's (1954) higher order needs of esteem, belonging and self-actualisation. He found that where workers have a voice in the decision-making process and are given responsibility, they find their work more challenging, satisfying and more likely to meet higher order needs, as they see tasks as their own rather than an imposition from others. Reward systems need to take these factors into account. Where employers simply distribute material rewards they tend to see employees as utilities – that is, as units with which to get tasks done rather than as people with higher order needs to fulfil at work.

> **Section summary**
>
> A simplistic, behaviouristic model of organisational reward systems holds that people work harder for greater extrinsic rewards. However, humans are active in assessing what they will contribute against what they receive. Incentive systems can reward on a group or individual basis and research shows that group rewards for co-operative behaviour create higher levels of achievement and productivity. Employers also need to consider intrinsic rewards for their employees and to recognise higher orders of human rewards such as self-fulfilment or actualisation.

## KEY TERMS

360 degree feedback
behaviourist model of reward
bonus incentives
collectivist culture
competitive goals
co-operative goals
critical incidents technique
development dialogues
employee voice
external and internal attribution
extrinsic and intrinsic motivation
functional job analysis
halo effect
position analysis questionnaire
incentive systems
individualistic culture
individualistic goals
inducements–contributions balance
information validity
inter-rater reliability
intra-rater reliability
job analysis
job components inventory
job samples
merit-pay incentives
performance appraisal
positive and negative reinforcement
punishment
rating scales
reliability and validity
work profiling system

EXERCISE **1a**

If your tutor permits, devise a questionnaire which will gather information on all that is involved in the job of lecturer or teacher. If not, do the same for a parent's or good friend's job.

Using the critical incidents technique interview a fellow student about the 'job' of being a student. For example, include questions like 'What was the last successful moment you experienced as a student? What factors produced it? What made it a success?' Similarly ask about bad moments too!

With a willing student colleague set up a performance appraisal interview that sensitively enquires about how their studies have gone over a recent period (say four weeks), what they have achieved, what they have so far failed to do, what went wrong etc. Then try to set achievable goals for them to attain over the next similar period. Ensure that they agree with the goals and try to be as specific as possible, e.g. 'By the end of the next three months you will have re-read and made notes on your Winter term lectures, prepared an outline design for your coursework and read at least three different chapters in preparation for coursework.' Have your colleague do the same for you.

Afterwards ask and answer the questions: did specifying goals make your task easier, more manageable? Did it help to review performance to see the achievements and the gaps to be filled? After further review at four weeks, were the goals achieved? Which were and which were not and why?

1. Describe the concept of job analysis. Compare and contrast different methods of gathering data on job contents.

2. Evaluate appraisal systems in terms of the advantages and problems involved in running them.

3. Describe the extent to which reward systems can encourage higher levels of performance.

# Further reading

Dipboye, R.L., Smith, C.S. and Howell, W.C. (1994) *Understanding Industrial and Organizational Psychology: An integrated approach*. Fort Worth: Harcourt Brace. (See pp.343–365.)

Furnham, A. (1997) *The Psychology of Behaviour at Work*. Hove: Psychology Press. (See pp.112–20.)

# Websites

http://www.shrm.org/
Society for Human Resource Management (US)

http://sol.brunel.ac.uk/~jarvis/bola/jobs/index.html
Comprehensive materials on job analysis including a description of critical incident technique at:
http://sol.brunel.ac.uk/~jarvis/bola/jobs/incidents.html

http://www-hr.ucsd.edu/~staffeducation/guide/
Guide to performance management and appraisal, University of California San Diego

http://www.devmts.demon.co.uk/apprsal.htm
Critical article on appraisal

http://newsvote.bbc.co.uk/hi/english/education/newsid_1149000/1149752.stm
BBC News article giving individual reasons why pay is not the main reward concern for would-be teachers

http://sol.brunel.ac.uk/~jarvis/bola/rewards/salary.html
Article on reward systems form BOLA – Business Open Learning Archive based at Brunel University

http://www.hrmguide.co.uk/index.htm
A business based 'Human Resource Guide' but with many links and interesting articles that are relevant to selection, motivation and so on.

# Group behaviour
# in organisations

## Introduction

Many of the issues studied in the psychology of work concern the behaviour of the individual. We look at motivation, job satisfaction, performance and rewards as they apply to the individual. However, behaviour at work takes place in a social context. We are all mostly engaged in group interaction, making decisions with others, agreeing, negotiating and unfortunately sometimes arguing. Organisational psychology can lean heavily here on research in social psychology, but the relationship has often been the other way around. A good deal of what the ordinary psychology student learns in the area of social psychology has, in fact, been developed by psychologists working in the field, in companies and other organisations investigating how teams work, how groups and teams form, operate, solve problems and make decisions, how attitudes are changed, how conflict is managed and so on. This chapter selects some of the more important areas in that world of research and focuses upon:

- Group decision-making strategies and pitfalls
- Team roles and team building
- Sources and management of group conflict.

## Group decision-making – strategies and pitfalls

### INDIVIDUAL VERSUS GROUP DECISION-MAKING

A common cry heard in the corridors of schools, colleges and offices is 'Oh no! Not another meeting!' Many people think that meetings are a waste of time. They would rather sort out problems and make decisions on their own or with a like-minded colleague. Committee meetings are often seen as 'all hot air' with the effective decisions usually made elsewhere (cynically, often beforehand by those in power).

Are groups better or worse at solving problems than individuals? Early work by Maier and Solem (1952) showed that group discussion gave members confidence that their solution was correct but did not guarantee a correct solution! On the TV show 'Who Wants to be a Millionaire?', when couples appear together, they often talk themselves into a wrong decision.

Maier and Solem also found that one group member with the correct answer will not always be heard and that for the group to be convinced it usually takes at least two people to argue the case. This finding squares with the work of Asch (1955), who showed that participants in his experiments were often influenced by a majority to agree with some quite obviously wrong solutions, for example that two obviously unequal lines were in fact equal. The 'majority' were in fact confederates of the experimenter, students trained to give the wrong answer. Just two confederates could exert considerable influence and three produced almost the highest levels of conformity found in the experimental trials, while larger numbers actually produced slightly less conformity. The effect has been replicated many times and into the contemporary era. Despite the fact that most people did not conform very often, resisting the answer favoured by the rest of the group felt very uncomfortable for most of the participants. The lesson here is not so much that we might accept wrong answers from our group, but that we might be inhibited from giving our own view.

Crutchfield (1955) showed that this effect would occur outside the laboratory and with questions for which there was no correct answer. He managed to get 37 per cent of US military officers to agree with the statement 'I doubt whether I would make a good leader' even though they had just been selected for military leadership training. Maier and Solem found that lower status individuals had less impact on group decisions. Asch showed that women and members of minority groups were more likely to conform to the group answer when their gender or minority status was emphasised by the nature of the rest of the group.

We should consider all these factors that inhibit group members from speaking out when we discuss the phenomenon of Groupthink below. We probably all can easily remember occasions where we knew we should say something yet kept quiet 'for a peaceful life'. However, here is a particularly alarming as well as sad example of how fatal group pressure can be. The extract (Brown, 1988) is an actual cockpit recording of an airline crew shortly before a crash:

Captain:    (*In a relaxed voice*) Well, we know where we are; we're all right.
Engineer:   The boss has got it wired.
Co-pilot:   I hope so.

| | |
|---|---|
| Captain: | No problem. |
| Co-pilot: | (*cautiously*) Isn't this a little faster than you normally fly this John? |
| Captain: | (*confidently*) Oh yeah, but it's nice and smooth. We're going to get in right on time. Maybe a little ahead of time. We've got it made. |
| Co-pilot: | (*uncertainly*) I sure hope so. |
| Engineer: | You know, John, do you know the difference between a duck and a co-pilot? |
| Captain: | What's the difference? |
| Engineer: | Well a duck can fly! |
| Captain: | Well said! |

This was in the last few minutes before the plane crashed. Here a majority of just two, including some seniority of rank, managed to silence a wise minority of one.

## THE RISKINESS OF GROUP DECISION-MAKING — GROUP POLARISATION

One might be forgiven for thinking that the committee is a very conservative, low risk arena. We imagine drab, grey-suited committee members using compromise and evasion rather than bold, brave decisions. However, classic work by Stoner (1961) showed that business students in groups tended to move towards more risky decisions than ones made by the individuals in those groups when asked alone. This was originally dubbed the **risky shift** phenomenon. However it was later shown that sometimes groups shifted to caution where group members were initially cautious as individuals (Fraser, Gouge and Billig, 1971).

### the Groupthink phenomenon

After the Paddington train crash in 1999 it emerged that there had been many reports and complaints by drivers about a difficult-to-see signal that was instrumental in the fatal tragedy. At Hatfield in 2000 railway personnel were aware of cracks in the rails many months before the crash that was eventually caused by them. The US space shuttle Challenger exploded on take-off in 1986 despite last-minute warnings by senior engineers.

'Groupthink', according to Janis (1982), occurs when a group's need for unanimous agreement on action prevails over the need for careful consideration of pros and cons and alternative possible actions. His point was that in the decisions preceding many disasters and calamitous political or business decisions, the consequences could and should have been anticipated. Janis might also have been interested in the decisions to go ahead with the Millennium Dome and to replace Wembley football stadium!

The symptoms of Groupthink are:

| | |
|---|---|
| Illusions of power | Group members underestimate the likelihood of their being wrong; they are unassailable and consider that they are morally correct |
| Closed-mindedness | Other views are not sought, they are not heard or they are belittled and attributed to a stereotyped out-group; negative evidence is ignored or explained away |
| Pressure to conform | Dissent is seen as disloyal; dissenters suppress their concerns; an illusion of unanimity occurs because of pluralistic ignorance – no objections means no problem; 'mind guards' hustle for support and keep bad or contrary news from their leader – see the engineer's behaviour in the flight crew example. |

In the Challenger disaster several of these factors operated. Political pressure to go ahead was powerful since President Reagan was due to talk with the first ever civilian aboard a space-flight, a schoolteacher who perished as her pupils watched the tragedy. Serious technical concerns were withheld from senior personnel. A one-third destruction of an O ring seal on previous flights was re-explained as a 'safety factor of three', given there was two-thirds left! Time after time the seal burn problem was considered in the light of growing evidence of danger and each time a new reason was found for it not to be considered critical. The day before launch the chief rocket engineer finally changed his mind and became a dissenter, but his views were neutralised by other authority figures.

Janis made some recommendations that, if followed, should help avoid Groupthink effects by keeping discussion open and being receptive to all views, doubts and alternatives:

- appoint devil's advocates to take contrary positions and raise questions
- permit members to discuss issues with associates outside the meeting (as far as security permits)
- form sub-groups to discuss policy aspects then re-convene
- allow a period of second chance reconsideration of doubts and alternatives
- leader (preferably impartial and not someone to follow) to encourage *all* members to speak their mind and encourage the airing of doubts and criticism: this should be done in an atmosphere of personal respect.

## MINORITY VIEWS

Although we have seen that those in a minority often find it harder to get their views taken seriously, nevertheless small groups do sometimes win round majorities. Moscovici (1985) conducted several studies of experimental groups with minorities primed to argue a contrary view. He concluded that, to succeed, minorities must *confidently* and *consistently* disagree with the majority even on issues other than the present case. The minority view needs to be realistic and consistently put. Nemeth (1986) argued that such minority views have the effect on the majority of getting them to reconsider their own, perhaps superficial, view of a debate.

Even if the minority view is wrong, Nemeth claimed that experimental groups make better decisions when exposed to them. For instance, the fuel protesters' campaign in September 2000 made many people think harder about the role of taxation in petrol prices. Many did not finally agree with the protesters but they probably had a clearer idea of why tax should be raised and what public services it should be spent on. A lesson for supervisors and managers then would be to encourage, not suppress, the expression of alternative views in the interests of creating broader, deeper, more creative thinking that may lead to better decisions.

> **Section summary**
>
> Individuals in groups can find it difficult to get their views accepted even if correct. Individuals can be influenced by even a small majority which holds an obviously incorrect view. Groups can polarise towards risky or conservative decisions, depending partly upon group members' original positions. 'Groupthink' refers to a dangerous tendency for groups (especially cults) to shut out alternative views, exaggerate supporting evidence and suppress dissent. Organisations can implement procedures to reduce the dangers of groupthink effects. Minorities can sway majorities and can, even if wrong, act as a healthy alternative voice in organisational debates.

# Team roles and team building

Most teams in the workplace are clearly identified – though one can find oneself being addressed as 'the team' without ever being told there was one or being invited onto it. Managers who talk about their 'team' are making an effort to get individual workers to realise that all their efforts are inter-dependent. If one person slacks, the rest must work harder, production is slowed down or another team is inconvenienced – see Theme link below.

An important organisational effect, demonstrated in many psychological experiments, is that of **social loafing**. The larger the number of people in a team, other things being equal, the less productive each individual becomes. This does not occur, however, where each team member's contribution can be identified or where individuals are made to feel that their contribution is important. It also does not occur in non-Western cultures termed 'collectivist' (e.g. India, Japan). Earley (1989) found that management trainees from China did not 'loaf' in larger teams whereas American trainees did. The reason is possibly because a sense of shared responsibility and duty to others is stronger in collectivist societies (Triandis, 1994). Erez and Somach (1996) tested two sub-cultures in Israel, one collectivist, the other individualistic. Even the individualistic group did not 'loaf' in larger teams when there were specific goals to achieve. Hence the researchers argue that the social loafing effect may be mainly confined to Western psychological laboratories. At work we know our team members, we can identify their contribution, at least in part, and we usually know what we are supposed to be doing (we have specific goals).

## TEAM BUILDING

Most organisations these days use some form of **team building** activity in order to motivate employees and make their working teams more effective. This is partly to offset those negative tendencies that can occur in groups which we have already considered, but it is also to heighten people's awareness of their dependence upon one another.

Furnham (1997) claims there is little empirical evidence that team-building procedures actually produce better performance or efficiency. One reason for this is that it is difficult to measure outcomes that apply to a whole team (as against individuals) in a field setting. Hence it is difficult to measure 'team success'. There are also very few measures of how people actually behave in teams. Most psychometric measures are of *individual* characteristics.

One classic self-assessment questionnaire of team roles was developed by Belbin (1993). He identified nine (originally eight) roles that are needed in a team. Usually some team members will perform more than one role or, in large teams, there can be duplicates, since not all teams have exactly nine people in them. The roles are given in Table 3.1.

• **Table 3.1:** Belbin's (1993) proposed general team roles

| Co-ordinator, chairperson | Calm, confident, steady, an impartial leader who encourages members to contribute, sums up group feelings and expressions and keeps the group focused. |
| --- | --- |
| Shaper | Energetic, driven achiever who concentrates hard on team goals and who pushes the group towards decisions and actions. |
| Plant | Innovative, creative and excellent thinker who contributes insight, new ideas and criticisms that lead to new solutions. |
| Implementer | A practical hardworking organiser who attends to detail and everyday tasks. |
| Team worker | Diplomat who helps keep up team morale, provides emotional support, offers advice and shows care. |
| Resource investigator | An outgoing, adaptable communicator who makes external contacts and seeks information to bring to the team; tends to start things rather than finish them. |
| Technical specialist | An expert who provides the team with specialist knowledge and experience. |
| Monitor, evaluator | Takes hard, logical approach to ideas and analyses in an unemotional, sober manner; interprets but does not inspire. |
| Completer, finisher | Orderly, conscientious planner who worries about last details in order to follow through ideas produced and often abandoned by non-completers. Can worry too much and not leave things alone. |

Where Belbin's questionnaire is used in team-building exercises, participants use the results to identify and discuss the roles they prefer and those they usually occupy. A very important aspect of such training is to get each team member to recognise and value the role of others, even if it is something they cannot fully understand or appreciate. Success in this leads to greater awareness of the interdependence of each team member on each other and can help people understand why their colleagues behave differently to the way that they themselves do. It might also reduce petty jealousies and help colleagues to see why some members should have different treatment which is not, in fact, preferential.

According to Furnham (1997) there is little psychometric evidence to support the validity or reliability of Belbin's measure of team roles (the Belbin Team-Role Self-Perception Inventory). According to Belbin's theory however, excellent teams require:

- A leader of the co-ordinator type who can see and use the strengths of every individual in the team in a patient manner. This person also needs to be able to generate the trust of others.
- A plant – for the novel solutions to problems in which the team is stuck.
- A range of thinking ability. Teams of academics, for instance, can spend far too long in debate and criticism and not get on with action, whereas the well-balanced team will have doers and finishers within it.
- A wide spread of the skills associated with the other roles in the model.
- Members who are in roles to which they are suited. It is no use having a shaper or a plant in a co-ordinator's role (e.g. a small group manager) when the diplomatic skills of patiently bringing every one into a project are required.
- An awareness of their own limitations. Remember the dangers discussed in the section on Groupthink. Self-aware teams can adjust for deficiencies by allocating members to missing roles and providing training where necessary to fill the gaps.

**Section summary**    In the West at least research has shown that team members work less hard in groups than when alone. Team building is used to raise awareness of team members' dependence upon one another, to focus upon the positive nature of each member's role and contribution and to generally increase cohesiveness. Belbin's team roles are a useful category system for analysing team contributions.

# Group conflict – sources and management

Conflict can occur *within* groups or *between* them. Conflict is, unfortunately, a fact of everyday working life. Everybody's needs and wishes cannot always be met and at some point there is bound to be a mismatch between what one group and another wants, or between management and employees. Looking at Belbin's team roles above we can see that conflict will inevitably occur *within* a team as the energetic, impatient shaper wants to forge ahead against the advice of the completer or co-ordinator.

Conflict is destructive at its worst. Consider the management team wishing to make cost cuts in order for the organisation as a whole to survive. Lower salaries are announced, longer hours and a few forced redundancies. The employees hold a protest meeting in work time. Everyday life is disrupted because everyone is angry or frightened. The productivity of the company decreases under this atmosphere of disruption and we begin a vicious circle in which no one can win. For these reasons, if no others, organisations need to study the sources of conflict and, more importantly, ways to manage it.

SOURCES OF CONFLICT AT WORK

Kabanoff (1985) produced an analysis of the work context which saw most conflicts as the result of an interaction of any two of the sources of influence on work teams listed below:

• **Table 3.2:** Kabanoff's sources of influence and conflict at work (1985)

| Source of influence | Description |
|---|---|
| Informal | Factors not part of the official organisational structure |
| Ability/knowledge | Skills and knowledge that members possess |
| Assignment | The position of people and jobs in the communication framework |
| Authority | The power attached to a role or person |
| Allocation | Tasks, time or resources officially allocated to positions, jobs |
| Precedence | Position or status of tasks or people |

Examples of conflict between any two of these sources might be:

*Allocation/Precedence*:    a group of secretaries argues that they should have new computers before the junior clerks receive them.

*Ability/Authority*:    a senior sales assistant who is promoted to a lower management position but has poor delegation, supervisory and diplomatic skills.

*Assignment/Allocation*:    a person from an isolated department who knows little of the rest of the organisation but is given the role of equal opportunities co-ordinator for the whole organisation.

Some specific sources of conflict, all of which can be related back to the categories above, are:

## co-operative vs. competitive goals and rewards

We saw in Chapter 2 that groups can be structured to work co-operatively or competitively. Where rewards are individual rather than group-based there is a strong source of potential conflict.

## interdependence of tasks

This conflict is heightened where the task of one individual or group is dependent upon another. For instance, where one group must work on a product only after a previous group has finished with it, there is a good chance of conflict.

## ambiguity

There can be ambiguity of role or task. Role ambiguity occurs where employees are not certain what is and is not a part of their job. A constant complaint among lecturers is that their job spills over into administrative tasks (such as creating and printing class lists, keeping records of marks) that could and should easily be performed by clerical staff. Task ambiguity occurs where it is not clear how a certain task should be performed.

## communication

We shall see in the next chapter that the systems of communication within or between groups can have a significant effect on the kinds of experience that individuals have and on the ways in which information percolates through to all members of the organisation – formally or via the grapevine. Lack of appropriate information by an appropriate time is a very frequent complaint. If one crucial piece of information does not arrive then employees might spend a lot of effort performing a task that is now not required or needs to be done differently. People feel particularly aggrieved if they find that their juniors know something before they do: a conflict of assignment and precedence on Kabanoff's system.

## MANAGEMENT OF GROUP CONFLICT

To start positively, not all conflict need be managed. According to Riggio (1990) there are potential benefits from a contained level of conflict which can:

- Stimulate and motivate workers; too little conflict can produce complacency.
- Create innovation through the search for solutions.
- Induce the consideration of opposing views – this can be educational and improve the quality of decisions.
- Relieve unexpressed tensions, bringing issues to the fore for discussion.
- Raise standards if teams take pride in their work and wish to beat others.

## solutions to negative conflict

Kabanoff suggests balancing up the conflicting sources of influence in Table 3.2. For instance, the secretaries can also be given new computers or promised the next order; the new manager can be re-trained or given less of a person-management role; the equal opportunities co-ordinator can be given time to meet people.

## co-operative working

Where intra-group conflict has become a worrying problem, organisation management often introduces some kind of team-building development as described earlier. One method often used to emphasise team members' dependence upon one another is Aronson's (1978) 'jigsaw' technique. Team members are given one piece of a puzzle and have to work with each other to discover the whole pattern. Only co-operation and sharing can produce a result for the group as a whole. Also relevant here is Deutsch's (1949) success with student co-operative groups (p.34) because in addition to working harder and being more productive, his students also liked each other more than the students working in competitive groups.

## the strength of group identity

One of the problems with trying to resolve conflict *between* groups is that groups form very strong identities. The work of Tajfel *et al.* (1971) showed that simply being allocated to a group on an arbitrary basis (e.g. the toss of a coin) led individuals to favour their own group when sharing out resources, even though they had not met their team members. They would also deny resources to other groups even where this meant that their own group would then receive less than they might have done. Note that the equity theory of motivation stresses the *difference* between our group and others as a motivating force, rather than the absolute amount we receive.

　　Earlier than Tajfel, Sherif *et al.*'s (1961) research seemed to demonstrate that competition for scarce resources *caused* group identity and cohesiveness. In these studies it was seen that when boys at a summer camp were divided into two teams they nevertheless maintained friendships with boys who had been selected for the opposing team. However, once competitions were started in which one team could win prizes only at the expense of the other, these friendly contacts broke down. Group cohesiveness became extremely powerful and a lot of aggression was expressed towards the other side.

## super-ordinate goals

Whether competition is necessary or not for groups to become hostile to one another, we need to find ways to lessen this hostility and to get separate groups to respect one another, especially in the workplace where animosity breeds poor work relations and inefficiency. Sherif *et al.* attempted conflict reduction by introducing a super-ordinate goal important to the whole camp (fixing a broken water tank or a broken-down bus taking them all to a movie). **Super-ordinate goals** are those that threaten members of more than one sub-group within an organisation. Very often it is the threat of redundancy or worsening conditions that will bring together parties who on a day-to-day basis are not on the best of terms. Evidence that external threat and super-ordinate goals can improve interpersonal relations comes from field research in a work setting where Stagner and Eflal (1982) compared USA Ford car workers who went on strike in 1976 with Chrysler and General Motor Company workers who did not. The Ford workers showed greater militancy, more support for their leaders and greater union participation.

In a study of West Virginian black and white coal miners, Minard (1962) found that group identities and norms *above* ground still largely determined typical group behaviour of non-integration (white miners lived and socialised separately from black miners). However, *below* ground, where all workers had the same overall goals, 60 per cent of white miners integrated with black workers. Hence some aspects of the conflicts occurring above ground were reduced through the common goals shared beneath.

## putting people together – the 'contact' hypothesis

When groups are in conflict, or are hostile to one another, a popular strategy is to bring them together in order to reduce stereotypes and let members of one group see what their enemies are really like, as individual humans. Sometimes this occurs, at work or at school, through the idea of a friendly competition, a discussion or a party. Research has shown that competitive events can easily *increase* hostilities and that there are certain criteria that must be met before there is any chance of conflict reduction:

- group members should not behave in ways which confirm the existing stereotype
- individuals need to be seen as typical of their group, otherwise they may not be seen as breaking the stereotype
- meetings should be informal so that personal relationships are possible
- there must be opportunity for members to do things co-operatively
- the environment should support co-operative behaviour and stereotype reduction; the effort will be unsuccessful where meetings are arranged by staff who only tacitly support the stereotypes or are obviously performing a token gesture
- members have equal status – this will be difficult in the workplace where, for instance, managers meet clerical staff, but efforts can be made to remove status signals such as uniform, formal titles, and so on.

Where groups discover that they are *indeed* very different then the attempt may well be doomed.

Group conflict has many sources and one way to analyse these is to look at clashes between different sources of influence. Not all conflict need be seen as negative or destructive. A limited amount can stimulate productivity and inventiveness, improve debate and ease tensions. Where conflict is destructive however, sources of influence can be balanced, groups can be brought to work co-operatively together, team-identity building can be implemented, super-ordinate goals can be introduced and contact can be increased between groups. In the last case though, several criteria need to be met before increased contact is likely to be effective.

## KEY TERMS

**conformity**
**contact hypothesis**
**co-operative vs. competitive goals**
**group conflict**
**group identity**
**group polarisation**
**groupthink**
**minority influence**
**risky shift**
**social loafing**
**super-ordinate goals**
**team roles and team building**

EXERCISE **1**

An old film worth seeing is 'Billy Budd' in which a much-loved and very simple-minded country boy, press-ganged into the British Navy in the late 18th century, is on trial for accidentally killing, under extreme provocation, an obnoxious and malevolent bully whom men and officers mutually despise. The officers seem unanimously agreed to avoid the death penalty until one man makes a clear and deeply persuasive argument concerning the reasons why they *must* hang the boy. Gradually all the others, very reluctantly, come round to this point of view.

Devise a scenario which involves an element of risk. Examples are: buying shares in a new dot.com company; a company considering taking over another; a wife/husband considering leaving their partner (include details of their potential new life); a person considering a change of career or a return to study. Make sure there are enough details to make the decision a difficult one with roughly equal advantages and disadvantages on either side. Ask individual members of a group *on their own* to give the level of risk they would tolerate to make a 'go ahead' decision from chances of success = 1/9, 3/9, 5/9, 7/9 or 9/9. Now ask the group to debate the issue and come up with a group decision on level of risk, *without declaring their original position*. Observe whether groups shift to risk or to safety. Have them discuss the reasons for their direction. (This exercise may require tutor assistance.)

If numbers permit have a group of eight to ten people try to solve a difficult task. Examples might be a charity event that really will raise funds; how to spend £10,000 to improve learning resources on our course; how to produce a coursework assignment where it is impossible for students to hand in another's work. Better still give the group some kind of difficult construction task. As the group works on the problem, the rest of the class act as observers and note which one of Belbin's roles fits each member. Discuss these observations with the group to see whether members readily accept your team role as typical for them or not.

1.  Discuss the extent to which groups can make poorer decisions than individuals, using research evidence to support your views.

2.  Critically evaluate psychological approaches to the reduction of group conflict.

# Further reading

Brown, R. (1999) *Group Processes* (2nd ed). Oxford: Blackwell.
Hogg, M. and Vaughan, G. (2002) *Social Psychology* (2nd ed). Englewood
  Cliffs, NJ: Prentice Hall.

# Websites

http://www.uiowa.edu/~grpproc/crisp/crisp.html
Centre for the study of group processes, University of Iowa

http://www.workteams.unt.edu/
Centre for study of work teams, University of North Texas

http://www.socialpsychology.org/
Social psychology network – extremely useful source for social psychology
  in general but cited here for its help with group behaviour and conflict.

# four

# Interpersonal communications systems

## Introduction

Changes in communication technology in the last ten years have had such a huge effect on organisations and society in general that it is probably still too soon to appreciate just how far-reaching are the effects. Just five years ago I became able to send files of information from my office to my home via e-mail. Suddenly the need even to copy onto disc and physically take files home was banished forever, let alone the need to print anything out. Nowadays I write a note to my sister in Australia and she receives it instantly (if she's awake at that hour!). If I'm not sure of a train connection, where to buy a caravan, who wrote The Hobbit, when the Tour de France starts and where it goes, I turn to the Internet. When e-mailing first got going at work I worried that we'd stop going round to each others' offices to talk to one another. Sure enough there is now research on this and, as we shall see later, at least one large company tried banning e-mails for a month just to improve face to face communication.

When social psychology researchers discuss communications in organisations they often refer to three aspects of a message-sending process: the *source* (who or what sent the message), the *channel* (the medium used to transmit the message) and the *audience* (those who receive the message). In the first section we shall look at some of the channels and various effects on them. In the second we shall look at the way the *network* of communication you are in (who can communicate with whom and how) affects the behaviour of yourself and others. To understand the possibilities here just think of the position of a young person who is the only person in their social group to possess a mobile phone. All messages would pass through them and they could choose who to connect to whom. Organisations spend a lot of time deciding who should communicate with whom in order to spread information efficiently and who should be barred from receiving messages or being able to talk directly to superiors. The chapter will end with suggestions about ways to improve communication flow within organisations, taking into account all the points in a communication chain. The section headings for this chapter then are:

- Types of communication channel and influences upon them
- Communication networks and cycles
- Improving communication flow.

# Types of communication channel

The medium by which we send a message may have a direct influence on how well that message is transmitted and upon the reactions of those for whom it is intended. It is possible to choose a wholly inappropriate medium for a message. For instance imagine an e-mail message from a good friend rather than a Christmas card. An Internet card, of course, might be a bit different.

Listed in the table below are the most common channels for communicating messages and then the aims of the messages. Which medium would be most appropriate for which types of message? (My suggestions are

• **Table 4.1:** Common channels for communicating messages

| Common communication channels | Aims of various messages |
|---|---|
| 1.  Telephone | Complex instructions about a task to be completed next week (4, 6, 9, 10) |
| 2.  Face to face | Mild disciplinary warning (late arrival at work) (2) |
| 3.  Meeting | |
| 4.  Written memo | Obtaining the team's agreement on a policy change (3, 8) |
| 5.  Letter | Moving an employee to a different department (4, 5, 2) |
| 6.  E-mail message | |
| 7.  Voice mail | Terminating someone's employment (2 + 5) |
| 8.  Formal report | Asking team to work harder towards an important deadline (3, 8, 4, possibly 6) |
| 9.  Video conference | Informing senior management about proposed changes to practice (3, 4) |
| 10. Formal notice | |
| | Confirming the time of a meeting (1, 4, 6, 7, 10) |

the numbers in brackets on the right-hand side).

Lengel and Daft (1988) suggested that the 'richness' of the medium should be the main basis on which to make decisions about how exactly to send a message. Richer media are those where multiple cues are provided and feedback can be very rapid. Face to face we can transmit all our usual non-verbal cues and can appreciate immediately the effect of our message on its target. A telephone call contains some of these aspects but no visual cues. A tutor can enrich a verbal message with good visual aids. Memos, e-mails or, at worst, public notices, contain decreasing levels of richness.

Suppose you were a student who had turned in a rather weak essay. Would you rather receive all the tutor's comments in written form, on your essay, or would you prefer a one-to-one meeting where the tutor takes you through positive and negative aspects? Most students would prefer the richness of the meeting, so long as the tutor had good social skills. The tutor can respond to misunderstandings and can reassure you when the going gets heavy, whereas with written messages only there is far greater potential for hurt feelings and unresolved distress.

In a work setting, Muchinsky (1977) found that workers were *more* satisfied with their jobs the *more* they had face to face contact with their supervisors. Satisfaction was negatively related to frequency of written communication – the *more* memos they got the *less* satisfied they were. Of course the causal direction is difficult to identify here – it could be that the poorer workers necessarily received more written instructions or warnings, rather than that dissatisfaction was caused by the written materials. However, managers must in general take great care over the nature and appropriateness of their messages and the media they use to transmit them. Hearing of an undesirable office move via a formal notice pinned to the wall is not likely to generate a well-motivated workforce. In such cases it would make a lot more sense to hold an open meeting, outlining all the positive aspects of the proposed change, with plenty of room for questions and discussion, in order to try and move towards acceptance and 'ownership' of the change by the staff team.

**Section summary**

Communications involve messages and these may be sent through various media or channels. Channels vary in their richness, a concept relating to the number of cues available and speed of feedback response. Job satisfaction has been related to channel richness as a mediating factor. Organisational communicators need to consider the appropriateness of the channel used for the particular type of message.

# Communication networks and cycles

## INFORMATION FLOW IN ORGANISATIONS

According to Riggio (1990) information in organisations can flow in three specific directions, *downward*, *upward* and *laterally*. The content of messages can also be *filtered* (some detail removed), *censored* (whole message blocked) or *exaggerated*, for instance by minimising the seriousness of a problem in upward communication from a supervisor to management or by dramatising the consequences of failing to meet targets (e.g. redundancies) in a downward message from supervisor to work team. Lateral (sideways) information flow can help in distributing important information on the job, support interpersonal relationships and increase productivity by helping in the co-ordination of work tasks, especially across departments. However too much informal lateral flow, such as general chat and gossip, can impede efficiency (Riggio, 1990).

O'Reilly (1980) found that workers who receive more downward information tend to be more satisfied. Downward communication includes the content of appraisal sessions (see p.27). Baird (1977) found that US companies were particularly low on this form of downward communication about work performance. Koehler *et al.* (1981) found that workers who were able to send more upward communications to their superiors were also more satisfied in their jobs.

## NETWORKS

A communication network is any system where people are in communication with one another, including upward, downward and lateral links. We have seen already (p.57) that where workers are *involved* in discussion and decisions, morale is usually higher. Early work investigating the relationship between group satisfaction and the level of participation in a communication network was provided by Bavelas (1969). His work made a distinction between 'centralised' and 'de-centralised' communication networks. The major patterns are shown in Figure 4.1. Arrows represent the direction of communication between members.

### centralised networks

The 'wheel' (in Figure 4.1) is highly centralised, since only the central person can communicate with other team members. This would be typical where a leader only talks with each team member one at a time or in a very formal meeting where all comments and points must be made through the Chair. The 'Y' is only slightly less centralised and is typical of the communication pattern of a conventional hierarchical structure – for instance, downward from Department Head to Deputy to ordinary group members. Note that ordinary members may only feed their messages back upwards through the Deputy.

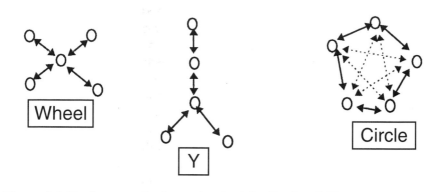

• **Figure 4.1:** Simple communications networks *(after Bavelas, 1969)*

## decentralised networks

The 'circle' represents the typical lateral flow of information round individuals (who work separately) in a work group or even round a set of departments or classes in a school. It also resembles the flow of messages around a group of separated friends each with a mobile phone. Where individuals work as a group, e.g. within an open office or an informal classroom, the circle would have the additional dotted lines shown in the figure, so that every member can communicate freely with all others, as in a democratic meeting, a relaxed office or in a social setting.

## differing networks – efficiency and satisfaction

Early experiments (e.g. Leavitt, 1951) showed that when groups of experimental participants were organised according to the patterns of communication shown in Figure 4.1, the less centralised groups took longer to establish a leader and were relatively unstable. Each member of a group had a card with five symbols on it and the group had to find which single symbol was common to all members. The less centralised groups performed worse on this task. However, they were superior on more complex tasks and expressed greater satisfaction with the experience. In the centralised groups the central participants enjoyed the task far more than the peripheral members and were usually selected as leaders. Since they were initially allocated to positions at random this shows that the *situation* (position in a group) rather than personality characteristics led to the role of leadership.

## grapevines and rumour

We have probably all encountered rumours in our daily lives (at least, of the kind that tell us who is going out with whom!). To what extent would you think the rumours you have heard turn out to be true? The word 'rumour' makes it sound as though most are incorrect but, in fact, Baird (1977) investigated the

Organisational structure and communication

The importance of organisational structure and consequent communication patterns could not be more gravely emphasised than by the launch explosion of the Challenger spacecraft in 1986, mentioned earlier. This was watched live by millions of television viewers including schoolchildren who knew that their teacher was aboard.

The US space-flight organisation NASA is huge and at that time had a structure in which there were many relatively independent decision-making teams. Very few decisions therefore made it to the top of the organisation, partly because it was believed that nothing would ever be resolved efficiently if all decisions had to be confirmed at the highest level. One member of the Presidential commission investigating the disaster said, 'It's so structured that communication is inhibited. No matter how big a problem is, there ought to be a top dog who is responsible.' (Newsweek, March 3, 1986, cited in Saks and Krupat, 1988)

Similar concerns about organisational communication and the stifling of crucial information have been raised concerning the UK train crashes in 2000 and 2001 at Paddington and Hatfield. Before the Paddington disaster, which killed 31 people, Railtrack (the track operating company) were sent three written warnings from a train operating company about 'signals passed at danger' near Paddington. Drivers had repeatedly complained about signal 109 which was difficult to see. The driver who passed the red signal on the day had not been told that the signal had been 'passed at danger' by other drivers eight times before the accident.

rumour system in an occupational setting and found that around 80 per cent of rumours turned out to be factually correct.

Rumours are sent around an informal circuit of communication known as a 'grapevine' and tend to flourish when there is a lack of information flowing through the formal network. Rather than attempting to stifle the grapevine, Baird argues, effective managers will attempt to tap into it and to publish accurate information well ahead of any opportunity for rumour to develop.

Communication on the grapevine, according to Baird, is determined by three major factors – *friendship*, *usage* and *efficiency*. Friends are more likely than others to transmit messages around the grapevine for the obvious reason that they like communicating with one another and will pass on a rumour as easily as any other type of information. People who are in the formal communication system (they are common *users*) will also be highly likely 'nodes' (joining points) in the grapevine network. A manager, for instance, will talk to his secretary and he or she may well then pass on the rumour via the circuit of other secretaries and administration staff. Finally, the grapevine is used where people find it *efficient*. 'Could you mention it to anyone you see today' may well be a quicker means of communicating an urgent matter than waiting to send the message through more formal channels. A final point from Baird is that grapevines serve an important role in maintaining social relationships in an organisation. It is a way of maintaining friendships and keeping workers together with a sense of unity and commitment to the workplace. Hence, any manager attempting to stifle the grapevine may risk generating serious ill-feeling whilst damaging a useful if not inevitable method of communication among the workforce.

Information flow in organisations can be upward, downward or **Section summary** lateral, including filtering, censoring and exaggeration. Various effects of these processes on worker productivity and satisfaction are mentioned. Organisations contain different sorts of networks of communication. Early research on people's behaviour within, and responses to, different kinds of network tended to show that centralised networks are more efficient for simple tasks but less efficient for more complex tasks. People at a controlling point in a network tend to be more satisfied than those at the periphery and more likely to be given leader positions. Grapevines can be efficient fact-carrying networks for informal messages within an organisation and can be used effectively by senior staff.

# Improving communication flow

Having considered the various forms and uses of communication, it is now possible to discuss methods of improving communication flow in an organisation by looking at the likely breakdown points in the transmission from sender to audience. Figure 4.2 shows the relevant stages in the communication process and we then go on to look at ways in which information flow can be improved, considering each point in Figure 4.2 in turn.

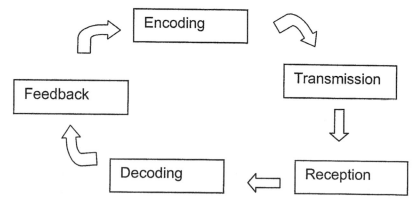

• **Figure 4.2:** Stages in the communication process

## encoding

It is important that sender and receiver both communicate at the same level. Different languages obviously pose a problem but so does the use of jargon familiar to one but not the other. Hence messages intended to travel outside an organisation or department need to be set in quite different terms from those transmitted within. Senders must also consider the medium and the potential for misunderstanding, for instance, trying to be ironic in an e-mail where there are no symbols to demonstrate irony. Consider the difference between 'I bet your staff are finding it easy,' and the same with '*I bet* …' in italics.

## transmission

As we have just seen, changes in the sense of a message can occur during its travel as a result of the method selected for its composition and transmission. Information can be *omitted*, *distorted* or *filtered* out. The game of Chinese whispers shows us just how much the sense of a message can change as it is passed on from person to person in a chain (in fact, we could see each person to person stage as a complete encoding-to-reception process). Bartlett (1932) used experiments to show that what gets maintained in a message are its important or outstanding features. Unremarkable parts may well be omitted. However, because humans need to pass on complete messages that make sense, they will tend to fill in any missing parts with content that appears to rationalise the message. Hence, the message '*Every staff member must attend the examinations briefing next Wednesday as there are substantial changes in light of the University's new regulations*' might become *distorted* to '*There's a meeting next Wednesday if you want some information on exams; I believe they're going to regulate invigilation to make it lighter*'. People will also filter out what they deem to be unimportant, even if it is in fact crucial in the view of the sender. Hence, improvements to communication include dealing with any factors that can produce loss of clarity such as noise, haste, over-reliance on memory. Complex messages delivered orally (e.g. in a meeting) need to be backed up with written material (paper or electronic). Staff who pass on messages need to be trained not to omit detail or radically rephrase wordings.

We mention in Chapter 8 that open plan offices were originally designed to improve communications between employees. However, findings have shown that such offices increase informal chat but do not necessarily improve formal communications. Nevertheless, organisations need to make it as simple as possible for workers to communicate with one another and to use the richest media, especially face to face. This includes simple things like producing a useful telephone directory which enables a worker to find a central help point in an unfamiliar department, rather than having to pick any name from a long list of people with unfamiliar roles thus wasting time and possibly annoying staff who are inappropriate for the level of enquiry.

## reception

The state and the context of the receiver is all-important in the efficient reception of messages. Why for instance do people permit the telephone to dominate over face to face meetings, allowing the phone caller to 'jump the queue' over those who wish to talk to the receiver in person? Rather than taking a rushed message and returning to a long-interrupted conversation, staff need to be trained either to divert calls or arrange to call back so that both messages can be received relatively clearly.

Messages need to stand out from the crowd to be noticed. In these days of e-mail messages a printed memo can sometimes appear rather serious. E-mail users will junk messages unread simply by reading the subject, e.g. 'new books offer from Rainforest.com'.

## decoding

Receivers' expectations can seriously distort the content of a message as they decode it. The Theme Link box below outlines our dependence on schemas (or schemata) in decoding information. As we saw earlier, where there is possible ambiguity, as in a brief written note, then there is scope for misinterpretation in line with our personal schemas and expectations. Hence communications need to be put into a clear context before moving onto detail – a good piece of advice for student essay writers!

## feedback

Anyone who has made a long-distance international call where there is a tiny delay in reception will know just how disconcerting this can be. In face to face communication, eye contact is vital for the sender to know that the message is at least being received and generally followed. On the telephone we rely upon sound feedback to know that the other person is following us. With written communications, replies may be tedious (though not with e-mail) but are essential for the communication process to be effectively completed. The sender at least knows that the message was received and may receive back information which initiates a further round of communication.

In general, we would assume from the earlier findings on information flow directions in organisations, that increases in both upward and downward flow would be beneficial, so long as there is not information overload and workers are not cynical about management messages. A lateral increase in communication would also be beneficial so long as it is directed towards efficiency on the job and not just increased opportunities to socialise (assuming there are already adequate opportunities in existence).

Theme link to cognitive psychology (**Communications**)

The study of schemata, frames and scripts in Cognitive Psychology can tell us an immense amount about how messages should be composed and received in order for the most accurate transmission to occur. As we saw, Bartlett's work demonstrated that people distort and then rationalise incompletely recalled messages. Work on schema theory (see Eysenck and Keane, 1995) has shown that information is far more easily received and understood if it is given within an appropriate context. Bransford and Johnson (1972) gave participants the following passage:

> The procedure is quite simple. First, you arrange items into different groups. Of course one pile may be sufficient depending on how much there is to do. If you have to go somewhere else due to lack of facilities that is the next step; otherwise you are pretty well set ... It is better to do too few things at once than too many. In the short run this may not seem important but complications can easily arise. A mistake can be expensive as well ... It is difficult to foresee any end to the necessity for this task in the immediate future, but then, one never can tell. After the procedure is completed one arranges the materials into their appropriate places. Eventually they will be used once more and the whole cycle will then have to be repeated ...

Participants who were told the script was about doing the washing found it easy to understand and recalled far more information from the passage than those not given the context. Good managers, like good tutors, always put the issue in context before delivering a new or complex set of ideas.

## the sudden evolution of e-mailing – a threat to human interaction?

E-mailing is a relatively recent but revolutionary form of communication by which we can send instant messages round the world to hundreds of people at once and receive replies within seconds. The obvious advantages within organisations are the speed, the ease and the reliability of message-sending, although most organisations have found that it is a gradual process to dispel fear and to get all staff checking e-mail on a regular basis. Use of e-mail has been associated with increased mental and physical stress (Watanabe, 2000). However, in education, Tiene (2000) found students were positive about on-line discussion and e-mail communications, compared with face to face tuition, and Gold (2000) found no difference in performance between groups tutored in a short experiment under one or other of these two conditions.

Many people have feared that e-mail will, apart from making written communications quicker and easier, have the negative effect of keeping people in their offices and stopping them from engaging in normal human interaction: asking questions of colleagues at work, dropping by their offices, arranging meetings and so on. Locke (1998) argues that throughout human evolution a central function of talking has been to create intimacy. Through talking we learn to trust one another and to see each others' strengths and unique qualities. Communicating mainly by e-mail removes this aspect of work interaction and, according to Locke, threatens to create a distrustful and depersonalised society.

Messages rushed off in a hurry can appear particularly blunt to the receiver and in many cases an equally blunt reply leads to the development of highly aggressive and abusive 'flame mail' messages. Gotcher (1997), reporting on a study of college lecturer and administrator e-mail behaviour, recommended training in both confidentiality issues and the expression of anger. Personally, I have had the unpleasant experience of trying to warn someone that they were replying to the entire staff body without realising it when they intended only to reply to the original sender. The reaction was extremely hostile and an abusive reply to me was then sent round to several hundred college staff!

## talk to each other! an experiment in not e-mailing colleagues

In 2001 the UK lottery company Camelot took very seriously the notion that e-mail use can diminish the quality of normal human interaction. An executive issued an edict – no more e-mails for four weeks. According to an article by Burkeman in The Guardian (20th June 2001) a Camelot spokesperson said: 'We needed to make staff more aware of other forms of communication. If there were elements of the business where you could talk face to face instead of sending an e-mail, we wanted to encourage people to do that.' Unfortunately the article did not report any specific effects of the exercise.

Communications can be improved by making changes at various points along the communication chain, especially at the stages of coding and decoding where our cognitive schemas can prompt us to misinterpret ambiguous material. The more ambiguity and interference there is during transmission the more a message may be distorted because of the cognitive process of rationalising fragmented material into a coherent whole. Improvement (increase) in upward, downward and lateral information flow might have beneficial effects on productivity and satisfaction under certain conditions. The advent of e-mailing has had profound effects on interpersonal encounters among staff to the extent that some fear a lack of face to face talk may result in distrust and depersonalisation.

**Section summary**

## KEY TERMS

audience
censoring
centralised and decentralised networks
channel (of communication)
decoding downward, upward and lateral
  information flow
encoding exaggeration (of message content)
feedback filtering
grapevine
(communication) network
reception richness (of communication medium)
schemas
transmission

### EXERCISE 1

Try the old game of Chinese whispers. You simply compose and
send a message to the first person in a chain by whispering it to
them. This works better if there is quite a bit of noise in the room
and one is not *too* intimate with one's whisper! Note how the
message has changed as it has passed along the chain, and where
and why these changes occurred.

### EXERCISE 2

A more formalised version of this simulates Bartlett's original
experiments. Compose a longish message with some unfamiliar
jargon or technical terms and some unusual aspects (odd requests,
amusing jargon and so on). There are two ways to proceed. Either
use a version of Chinese whispers with each person telling the next
(not whispering) the message. Each receiver writes down their
version of the message then says this aloud to the next person in
the chain and so on. An alternative method is to have people try to
recall the story, writing their version down each time, over periods
of say, 30 minutes, then an hour, two hours and so on up to what is
practical (Bartlett used recall at weekly intervals in some cases).
Observe, either for the individual repetitions or for the human chain,
how salient features remain, how each version remains a relatively

coherent (but sometimes very odd) message and how unusual terms sometimes get retranslated into more familiar ones. Concepts unfamiliar to one's culture (which can just mean the culture of the organisation) can get reinterpreted as more familiar concepts within one's culture.

## EXERCISE 3

Work in pairs sitting back to back. One person in each pair holds a simple abstract design and has to tell their partner what to do in order to duplicate it. Note how important clarity, precision and accuracy are with this non-visual channel of communication.

## ESSAY QUESTIONS

1. Discuss the ways in which different types of communication network can affect the behaviour of people within them.

2. Evaluate the contribution that cognitive psychology can make to our understanding of the ways in which messages can become mistranslated.

## Further reading

Locke, J.L. (1988) *The De-Voicing of Society: Why we don't talk to each other anymore*. New York, NY: Simon and Schuster.
Riggio, R.E. (1999) *Introduction to Industrial and Organizational Psychology* (3rd ed). London: Prentice Hall International. Chapter 8, Communication in the Workplace.

## Websites

http://www.analytictech.com/mb021/commstruc.htm
For more detail on the Bavelas-Leavitt experiments

# five Leadership and management

## Introduction

Try to think of someone who has held a position of leadership over you and whom you have been very happy to work for. This might be a team leader in sports (e.g. a football captain), a task group leader (e.g. a camp leader in Brownies) or simply someone you know in a group of friends whom most people were happy to follow or take an example from. What is it about this person that made them able to lead, able to organise a group effectively, and made you happy to be in the group and to work for it?

In the world of work, organisational psychologists are interested in the sort of person whose style of leadership can keep a group together and make it productive, preferably whilst also maintaining a good deal of satisfaction among the group members. Moghaddam (1998) defines leadership as: '(the) process by which one person directs group members toward the attainment of specific goals' (p.455). What makes someone good at this? Perhaps we should break this question down into more basic queries:

- What features and characteristics mark out effective leaders as different from others?
- To what extent are these features 'natural' or developed?
- What factors in the situation help or hinder effective leadership?
- To what extent can leaders *learn* to be more effective?

Notice that we have introduced the term 'effective' here as we are not just interested in *any* group leader (e.g. a parent) but in leaders who get tasks carried out efficiently, productively, smoothly and with the least damage to future work relations among staff. In this chapter we shall look at:

- Theories of leadership
- Leadership styles
- Leader–worker interaction and satisfaction.

# Theories of leadership

## LEADER-CENTRED THEORIES

### great man theories

Many people just assume that great leaders were born to lead. The assumption is that Gandhi, Nelson Mandela or even Hitler, would naturally have risen to lead, even though the contemporary context is quite different from that in which they rose to power. In psychology such views are known as *great man theories* of leadership, but few contemporary psychologists would support them. Such theories are not of much use in the study of organisations since many people, with a variety of personal characteristics, get promoted into management or leadership positions regardless of whether they are 'great' men or women, but simply on the basis of their experience and skills. Social scientists have been more interested in what skills and characteristics are associated with effective leadership, and the extent to which these skills can be acquired.

The early psychological theories tended to focus on the leader *in isolation* – either their personality traits or their behaviour – and tended largely to ignore the role of the particular situation a leader had to lead in, the types of task to be completed and their relationship with the group members they were leading.

### trait theories

These theories see effective leaders as people possessing a high level of certain personality characteristics ('traits'), such as intelligence or self-confidence. Though early studies tended to assume that personality predicted leadership, later studies generally provided little evidence in terms of correlations between characteristics and effective leadership (see Hollander, 1985).

### universalist theories vs. behaviour theories

Both great man theories and trait theories are also known as **universalist** theories because they search for one or a few key characteristics of leadership assuming that people with these characteristics are highly likely to be successful leaders whatever the circumstances. They are criticised as being *reductionist* in that they *reduce* leadership to these characteristics.

In the 1950s attention turned away from specific personality traits and towards the types of *behaviour* that effective leaders displayed. Here, although of course it is possible that a certain *type* of person might generally use a consistent *type* of leadership behaviour, a major implication is that leaders (e.g. managers) can *change* their dominant style, they can be *trained* to use different and perhaps more effective *leader behaviour*. Also, we can look for competence in such behaviour in those we seek to appoint to manager/leader roles.

## CONTINGENCY THEORIES – TAKING THE CONTEXT INTO ACCOUNT

The early leader-centred theories described above, including those focusing on leader behaviour rather than universal characteristics, generally failed to find one type of effective leader *or* style of leadership behaviour. This is probably because it is unlikely that one set of characteristics will be effective for all leaders in all circumstances. Later research turned towards a consideration of the *situation* and the *task* required in determining the factors associated with effective leadership.

**Contingency theories** are those which take into account the *interaction* between the characteristics of the leader and their behaviour along with the features of the situation. It is no use, for instance, sticking slavishly to the principle and plans for getting the task done if your team is finding the going hard or constantly grumbling about the way you are leading them. An effective leader must at least be flexible and watch for such conflicts. These theories will be investigated in more detail in the final section of this chapter.

> Leadership theories can be roughly divided into two broad categories – leader-centred theories, which concentrate solely on the qualities of the leader, and contingency theories which also take into account various aspects of the situation – especially the task and relationships between leader and followers. Among the former are great man theories (never very popular in mainstream psychology), trait theories and behaviour theories. Various contingency theories will be investigated in later sections.
>
> **Section summary**

# Leadership styles

We look now at ways in which the general theoretical approaches outlined briefly above have been applied in identifying leadership styles and in investigation of the interaction between.

## LEADER BEHAVIOUR – FOCUSING ON THE TASK OR THE PERSON

The emphasis on leader *behaviour* is exemplified early on in the work of Lewin, Lippitt and White (1939) who trained leaders of boys' club groups to run activities, making models and papier-mâché masks. They submitted each of the boys, working in groups, to three different leadership styles:

| Democratic | Autocratic | Laissez-faire |
|---|---|---|
| Discussed possible projects with the boys and involved them in decisions about activities. Explained his comments. | Issued orders and *told* the boys what to do. Did not invite their opinions. Sometimes praised or blamed. Did not explain his comments. | Left the boys to themselves after instructing them to do the same as the others. Offered help only when asked. Did not praise or blame. |

Although it is generally believed that a democratic style of leadership is best, no one style in this study proved to be consistently superior in all aspects. The democratic style produced greater satisfaction among group members, yet the autocratic style produced either equal or even better models. However, the boys stopped working in the absence of the leader and fought far more. The third group displayed low morale and little productivity. Meade (1967) found that in India the autocratic style produced better results. It is always important to remember that most psychological results are produced in the West, mainly in the USA, and that each effect reported may well not generalise across cultures.

## THE EARLY OHIO AND MICHIGAN STUDIES

The methodology adopted by the researchers at Ohio University (the Ohio studies) was to administer questionnaires to both leaders and their subordinates. The major findings were that two major dimensions seemed to account for the majority of leadership behaviour. These were (Fleishman, 1969) **initiating structure**: the extent to which the leader defines roles and directs activity through planning, communicating, innovating and so on, and **consideration**: the extent to which the leader is concerned with establishing good rapport among group members, and with the promotion of mutual trust, respect and consideration of their feelings.

The Michigan studies, by contrast, concentrated on observing the differences between effective and non-effective leaders, finding that the former were more **relationship-oriented** – they took into account the feelings and views of their subordinates, involving them in some of the decision-making. Other leaders tended to focus solely on the task to be achieved. Though these became known as **task-oriented** leaders, the description is very similar to that of the 'initiating structure' described above. In the same way, 'relationship orientation' is very closely connected with 'consideration'. However, whereas the Ohio studies simply identified two types of leadership, the Michigan studies claimed that relationship-oriented leaders were more effective. In fact, studies tended to show that where leaders were high on one or other of these factors, group performance tended to be high, but that relationship-oriented leaders tended to produce more satisfied workers who stayed longer in the job.

## TRANSACTIONAL AND TRANSFORMATIONAL LEADERS

Because the Michigan and Ohio groups produced ambiguous results, with two types of leader at least appearing to be effective, later attention turned towards the *interaction* between the leader's style and features of the particular work situation – we will deal with that work in the following section. However it is worth noting here that, from the 1980s onwards, the pendulum has to some extent swung back again towards a focus on particular personality qualities in leaders, in particular the contrast between so-called **transactional** and **transformational** leadership qualities (Burns, 1978) which are outlined in Table 5.1.

• **Table 5.1:** Transactional and transformational leadership qualities

| Transactional | Transformational |
|---|---|
| Leader believes leadership is achieved via exchange (a transaction). Leader assumes people will follow only if there is something in it for them – a reward, an end result, team or individual success. | Leaders get followers to achieve beyond their expectations by using charisma, inspiration, self-sacrifice and the setting of clear, optimistic and apparently attainable goals. The leader takes into account individual strengths and encourages free-thinking and team spirit above personal concerns. |

House (1977) concentrated on **charismatic leadership** which includes the ability to influence others' beliefs and behaviour through the leader's own strength of belief, personal example and faith in their subordinates. House *et al.* (1991) conducted a study on US presidents using historical data, and attempted to show that a leader's need for power predicted their charismatic qualities which in turn predicted their success in the presidential position (leader effectiveness). Examples of charismatic leaders would be Martin Luther King or John F Kennedy. In the UK, John Major would count as non-charismatic while Margaret Thatcher and Tony Blair will probably be recalled as charismatic.

Bass (1985) used subordinates' assessments of their feelings about their leaders to measure aspects of transformational leadership, using a scale known as the Multifactor Leadership Questionnaire (MLQ). Bryman (1992) produced evidence that charisma and inspiration were related to positive effects on work performance.

However, Alimo-Metcalf and Alban-Metcalf (2000) query the general research evidence on transformational or charismatic leadership, arguing that much of it has been based on executives or 'distant leaders', as compared with the far more common 'nearby' leaders who are our regular line managers in the world of work. They also point out that the leaders researched are almost entirely male and there has been a concentration on subordinates' perceptions of their leaders. The Metcalfs' research includes female and male NHS and local government managers' perceptions of their own roles at a variety of levels. From these data they have developed the Transformational Leadership Questionnaire which, they argue, introduces more variables into the concept of transformational leadership. In particular, they found that while the US research emphasised the leader 'acting as role model', their own measure emphasised 'what the leader can do for his/her followers' (p.16).

**Section summary**    In the mid 20th century leadership theories focused (under the influence of the behaviourists) on leadership behaviour – what leaders actually *do* – rather than what leaders were *like*. Both the Ohio and Michigan studies, using different methods, identified two contrasting patterns of leader behaviour: initiating structure vs. consideration and task-oriented vs. relationship-oriented. The Michigan researchers favoured the relationship-oriented leader as more effective, though later research found people high on either dimension could be effective. Although research then turned towards contingency theories, which take account of the situation and features of the led group, transformational leadership theories have emerged over the last 15–20 years and remain influential in their emphasis on 'charisma' and inspirational qualities.

# Leader–worker interaction and satisfaction

Some of the major models of leadership have been left to this point since they involve the *interaction* between leader style and the context in which leadership will be attempted. The 'context' includes variables such as the type of task, the urgency of the situation and the existing relationships between leader and team.

Even the earliest studies of leadership behaviour, including Lewin *et al.*'s, tended to demonstrate that a *democratic* style of leadership, emphasising the participation of and interaction between group members and the leader, produce greater satisfaction among group members. Part of the success of transformational leaders might be their delegation of responsibility and their involvement of all members in the decisions and tasks of the group. One might suspect that such leaders, who trust their co-workers and show confidence in them, are more likely in most situations to have satisfied and productive working teams. That appears to be the overall finding from

**contingency theories**, those which take into account the qualities and style of the leader as well as the features of the team and the task situation to be dealt with.

## CONTINGENCY THEORIES – TAKING THE CONTEXT INTO ACCOUNT

### fiedler's model – the least preferred co-worker (lpc) measure

Fiedler's early model makes an underlying but basic assumption that good leaders need to be positive towards all team members, even those whom many would find intolerable to work with. This develops the theme of consideration and relationship-oriented behaviour from the behavioural models described earlier. Fiedler (1967) developed a measure of person orientation known as the **Least Preferred Co-worker** (LPC) scale. This asks people to assess the person they have found it most difficult to work with (their view of a 'poor' worker) on various person descriptions such as 'boring–interesting' or 'friendly–unfriendly'. Where leaders assess even people they don't much like working with quite positively, they tend to be high on consideration, whereas low scorers tend to be high on structure. Whereas the earlier behavioural approaches tended to assume that a leader could train to be better at the style on which they were originally weakest, an implication of Fiedler's model here is that consideration and structure are two opposite ends of one sliding scale. Hence, on this view, if you are high on one you are inevitably low on the other. A further implication of the Fiedler theory is that high LPC leaders are more complex in their thinking and leadership behaviour since they can make distinctions between work performance and personal qualities – they can separate their emotional reaction to colleagues from their assessment of their abilities. Low LPC leaders find this separation hard – they find it difficult to like or show warmth towards poorer workers.

Fiedler's theory assumed that leaders were pretty well stuck with their particular leadership style (i.e. they stayed close to their original LPC score). Remembering that contingency theories take the leader *and the situation* into account, Fiedler's research investigated the relationship between LPC scores and various situations in which a leader might have to make headway in getting the group to complete a task effectively. If leaders tend to maintain roughly the same style then the most effective way to get a group to complete a task will be to match the right kind of leader to the particular features of the task at hand.

Fiedler's research identified three main factors in the work environment which could have an effect on how well a leader manages a group performing a task:

**Leader–member relations:** the extent to which the leader is liked, respected and trusted by his or her team members and the confidence of the leader in the team.

**Task structure:** the extent to which goals are clearly defined, along with the procedures required to achieve these goals. 'Structure' is what students often appreciate when setting out on an assignment. If they know what exactly is required and exactly how they have to go about completing the assignment, they are a lot more confident and motivated to perform the tasks well.

**Position power:** the amount of power involved in the leader's role, including the power to administer rewards and punishments, to discipline and even to take on or release group members. Power can be high because the organisation formally lends weight to the role (e.g. teacher, manager) and will back up decisions made within the organisation's guidelines for the job. However, leader power can also be strong where the leader is unofficial yet highly respected by group members, e.g. the charismatic gang leader or the accepted leader of freedom fighters.

All three of these variables could, according to Fiedler, exist as high or low in value, with task structure being referred to as 'structured' or 'unstructured' accordingly. This being so it is possible to draw up a table of possible leader–task situations as shown below. Table 5.2 takes all possible combinations of 'high' and 'low' in the three variables and the better of these are termed 'favourable' situations whereas the poorer ones are 'unfavourable'.

• **Table 5.2:** Favourability of possible leader–task situations

| | High | ← | | Situation favourability | | → | | Low |
|---|---|---|---|---|---|---|---|---|
| | 1 | 2 | 3 | 4 | 5 | 6 | 7 | 8 |
| L-M relations | Good | Good | Good | Good | Poor | Poor | Poor | Poor |
| Task structure | Structured | Structured | Unstructured | Unstructured | Structured | Structured | Unstructured | Unstructured |
| Position power | Strong | Weak | Strong | Weak | Strong | Weak | Strong | Weak |

Now, the question is, which of these eight differing situations would require a high LPC (person-oriented) leader and in which would a task-oriented leader get the task done more effectively? According to Fiedler's research a *low* LPC leader is most effective when the situation is either *highly favourable* or *highly unfavourable* (situations 1,2,7 and 8), whereas a *high* LPC leader does better with the team when the situation is more *moderately favourable* (situations 3-6). Why might this be? Surely a good situation demands a good leader and wouldn't we have thought that a bad situation in particular would require a 'considerate' leader? Have a look at the next two situations for an explanation.

Uptown High football team just love and admire their coach (1), she is the school Head of Sports (2) and the team are focused on winning the forthcoming cup final match with the Downtown Upper School first XI (3). Do they really need a high LPC leader? They don't need someone to improve morale or be sensitive to members. They could probably cope with a non-person-oriented (low LPC) leader who would be able to focus entirely on the task and help them to win. According to Fiedler, when the situation is that good, high LPC leaders bend their behaviour towards the less dominant style of being task-oriented. Trouble is, the low LPC leader is already better at this and the high LPC leader is not so effective 'out of role' as it were. Here, a different 'considerate' coach might try to concentrate on the training and the strategy, but might also become distracted by any personal difficulties experienced by team members, even where these are not too serious, thereby failing to concentrate the players on the tasks. The team really only needs a 'doer'.

> Uptown Rovers for the cup – a highly favourable situation

(1) High Leader–Member Relations (2) Strong Power (3) Highly Structured Task

MWCC are led by someone who is just about tolerated by the team (1). He is the local butcher and volunteered for the task many years ago (2). At present the team is struggling for cash. They have decided that they need to generate a better image for the team in order to attract a local business into sponsorship but they have little idea how to go about doing this (3). Here, Fiedler would argue, a nice 'caring' leader may get nowhere and be (further) disdained by the team, whereas a task-oriented leader has nothing to lose and can at least direct the team towards the task in a situation of crisis. Again, when the relationship-oriented leader tries in this situation to concentrate on their less dominant style of task focus, they tend to fail and become even less respected while still having no legitimate power to wield.

> Much Whopping Cricket Club – a highly unfavourable situation

(1) Low Leader–Member Relations (2) Low Power (3) Relatively Unstructured Task

There is much research support for Fiedler's model. Peters et al. (1985) for instance conducted a very thorough meta-analysis. This is a study which analyses statistically the results of a relatively large number of similar studies where these can be directly compared. The overall results showed that

Fiedler's data do support the theory very well and that subsequent research data also provide a moderate fit, more so in laboratory than in field studies. However, they also concluded that more features of the situation probably need to be taken into account, for instance the length of the leader–member relationship. Later research suggests that short-term tasks benefit from highly task-oriented leaders, but the longer the team is in existence the more a high LPC leader is required. A fairly recent meta-analysis (Schriesheim *et al.*, 1994) found that the middle situations of Table 5.2 do give high LPC leaders the advantage, particularly so in situations 5 and 6.

Fiedler's later **Cognitive Resource Theory** (Fiedler, 1995) holds that intelligence and experience also have an impact on leadership effectiveness. Conditions of high stress occur in unfavourable situations, but also as a result of pressure from the leader's own managers. Stress produces overload and this in turn inhibits cognitive ability – i.e. makes it hard to think clearly. In such circumstances leaders employ old habits. Therefore leaders with greater experience should perform better. The idea is that when we are under great stress we tend to do things that come more automatically and are poor at thinking creatively. Cognitive resources are therefore another variable, along with the situation and accompanying stress, which should be taken into account when appointing a leader to a team and a task.

## the vroom & yetton decision model (1973)

Whereas Fiedler's models assumed that each leader's style tends to remain much the same, the Decision Model argues that leaders are decision-makers who need to select an appropriate leadership style, having taken into account the particular demands and qualities of the task situation. The styles that can be used are in the following range:

| AI | AII | CI | CII | GII |
|---|---|---|---|---|
| Autocratic style | Minimal consultation | Individual consultation | Group consultation | Full participation |
| Leader decides using undisclosed information. | Leader decides alone using information gathered from subordinates. | Leader decides alone after sharing problem with subordinates *individually* and obtaining their advice. | Leader decides alone after sharing problem with whole group and obtaining their advice. | Leader shares the problem with subordinates and the group decides collectively. Leader accepts the group decision. |

The model specifies a progression of decisions that leaders should make in order to select the most appropriate style for the particular situation. The factors to be considered include the time frame of the decision (urgent? long term plan?), the need for subordinates to 'own' the decision, the structure of the problem and so on. Consider how a student would feel if their tutor made an autocratic decision about how the class would celebrate after examinations were finished. Then compare this with what students would expect of their leader when deciding how best to teach a topic to students with widely varying levels of experience in the subject area.

Much research supports the model including Vroom and Jago (1978). They showed that a large proportion of managers' actual decisions were successful where they coincided with what the model would recommend, whereas only a small proportion were successful where decisions did not conform to the model. The model is unrealistic however, in that managers/leaders rarely have the time to go through a complex decision tree 'on the run'. Nevertheless it is possible that the model does in fact mirror the kinds of decisions that managers make in their everyday work. It could be that experience leads effective managers to make these decisions without the need for conscious deliberation. To consciously submit all the factors to a formal decision-making process might be too artificial, too time-consuming and too distracting.

## leader–member exchange theory

The theories so far considered have all assumed that leaders interact in a fairly uniform manner with all their subordinates. However, reality tells us that this is far from the case and that a manager will respond differently to different people. They may have quite close and rich relationships with a few trusted and liked people but rather more distant and less frequent interactions with newer, more 'difficult' or simply ill-fitting individuals in the team. The 'exchange' model proposed by Dansereau, Graen and Haga (1975) concentrates on how each individual leader–member exchange affects the subordinate's job performance, rather than looking at the performance of the group as a whole. This approach also implies that in order to improve leader effectiveness one should try to improve the quality of individual leader–member relations. Attempts to train leaders to do this have generally been successful. Scandura and Graen (1984) showed that training leaders to listen and to give subordinates a clear idea of what was expected of them led to significant increases in productivity and in workers' job satisfaction.

**Section summary** Contingency theories take into account the situation the leader works in. Fiedler's early theory considered member relations, the nature of the task and the power of the leader. Where a combination of these conditions makes the leadership situation either very favourable or highly unfavourable, a low LPC leader is likely to be more effective, where LPC ('least preferred co-worker') score measures leniency towards poor workers. High LPC scorers are effective leaders in the majority of typical and non-extreme leadership situations. Fiedler's later theory recognises the leader's experience and cognitive abilities and his theories are supported by substantial research. Vroom and Yago's theory claims that manager/leaders should use different strategies for different situations and that they can be trained to do so. Exchange theory emphasises the quality of interaction between leader and each individual group member, claiming that effectiveness is achieved through training leaders to react sensitively to individual member's needs.

## KEY TERMS

autocratic leadership style
behaviour theories of leadership
charismatic leadership
cognitive resource theory
consideration
contingency theories
democratic leadership style
favourability
initiating structure
laissez-faire leadership style
leader–member exchange theory
leader–member relations
least preferred co-worker (LPC) measure
person-oriented leadership style
position power
relationship-oriented leadership style
task-oriented leadership style
task structure
trait theories
transactional and transformational leadership
vroom & yetton decision model

# EXERCISE 1

Split (a class) into two groups and have each group elect one famous person whom most of the group admire for their great leadership qualities, e.g. Nelson Mandela, Gandhi. (This exercise could also be performed by just two people). Each group must then list all the qualities that they think made that leader so great, respected and listened to. Now meet as a whole group and list these features for each other. Discuss those that are common to both and those that are unique. To what degree do the lists agree? Which of the characteristics seem to be essential and which just peripheral or irrelevant to great leadership? Discuss other emerging issues but finish by trying to answer the question – was each leader truly a 'great man' or 'great woman' or could other people have led as well, given the circumstances?

# EXERCISE 2

Have two volunteers from your class/group learn how to make a simple Meccano or Lego model (or similar). The task will be for each leader to take a small group of people and get them to build the model but under two different instructional styles as follows:
At the end of this experience discuss the feelings of each group

| Democratic leader | Authoritarian leader |
|---|---|
| • Show the group a design or photo of the model, or the real thing if possible.<br>• Ask group members which parts they would like to do as the model grows, emphasising that everyone must have a go at some point (so the least confident can choose easy bits like putting wheels on).<br>• Make suggestions as the model progresses such as 'why don't you try doing X before Y?' and so on.<br>• Give lots of encouragement ('don't worry, you're doing fine' and so on). | • Start building the model by telling each person or small group in turn what they should do.<br>• Give no clue as to the nature of the finished model or design.<br>• Do not offer help when things go wrong but eventually tell the person what is wrong, and to undo that part. Ask the next person to carry on from that point.<br>• Do not offer encouragement at any time.<br>• If asked questions at first find words that amount to 'just get on with it' then, if difficulties continue, proceed as above. |

member and compare reactions to the two different types of leadership style.

These exercises may require tutor assistance.

## ESSAY QUESTIONS

1.  Discuss factors in the leadership situation that may affect or improve worker satisfaction and productivity.

2.  Critically assess theories of leadership and leadership style which do not take into account the situational context for leadership.

## Further reading

Arnold, J., Cooper, C.L. and Robertson, I.T. (1998) *Work Psychology: Understanding Human Behaviour in the Workplace*. London: Financial Times/Pitman Publishing. Chapter 14.
Hollway, W. (1991) *Work Psychology and Organizational Behaviour*. London: Sage. Chapter 7.

## Websites

http://www.ee.ed.ac.uk/~gerard/MENG/ME96/index.html
Good notes on leadership pages in the unlikely site of the Department of Electrical Engineering at the University of Edinburgh.

http://cls.binghamton.edu/
State University of NY centre for leadership studies – huge library of leadership articles but hard copies must be sent for.

# six

# Motivation to work

## Introduction

If you have ever worked in an organisation you may have noticed that some people seem 'driven' by their jobs, working hard and almost always performing well, while others seem to be there just for the money. Some people thoroughly enjoy their work, while others seem to hate coming in and are eager to leave as soon as they can. This is a serious management problem of course because if there are 'freeloaders' who work little while others work hard, and if there are dissatisfied employees who care little for the job, there will be conflict and threats to efficiency. Intuitively we must feel that motivation and satisfaction are strongly related. The more satisfying one's work, the harder one works, although perhaps one of the satisfying things about a job might be that it does not entail too much hard work and stress. Alternatively, perhaps the more motivated one is (for example by good, valued rewards) the more one derives satisfaction. How has psychology contributed to the study of motivation and job satisfaction? We shall look at major theories and findings in the next two chapters starting with the topic of motivation – what drives people to perform or to do better? In this chapter we will study:

- Theories of motivation
- How we might expect to improve work motivation
- The association, if any, between motivation and actual job performance.

# Theories of motivation

It will help to make two major distinctions before we start:

- Needs and wants: several motivation theories are based on the concept of *need* which refers to those things we cannot function properly without. Eating and drinking are obvious needs. *Wants* are things we do not need but would dearly like, for instance, a television, car, holiday. The line between needs and wants is hard to draw and is culturally defined. Do we need or do we simply want a car to get to work? More importantly, do we have a need to satisfy our personal ambitions? Is there a need for *self-actualisation* (see Maslow below) or is this a Western luxury, something only considered by those with the benefits of extensive education and job choices?

- Extrinsic and intrinsic motivation: **extrinsic motivation** refers to those things that are tangible rewards for work and which are not directly involved in the work itself, for instance the rewards of money, holidays, social contact with other workers. **Intrinsic motivation** is a drive from rewards integral to the job itself, for instance, a sense of worth, mastery of the tasks, satisfaction in completing one's work.

# Maslow's hierarchy of needs

Maslow's theory (1954) is extremely well known and proposes that people have five levels of need with the most basic at the lowest level of this list:

**Self-actualisation needs**: this is a term specifically related to the psychological school of humanistic thought (see Theme link box) and refers to attaining one's maximum potential for self-fulfilment. Obviously this is entirely in the area of *intrinsic* motivation, whereas the first three levels of need below are almost entirely *extrinsic* factors in terms of work motivation.

**Esteem needs**: need to gain the respect of others and oneself; feeling one is worthwhile and valued.

**Social needs**: need to have friends, be liked, be accepted.

**Safety needs**: security from physiological or psychological threat or harm.

**Physiological needs**: basic needs for survival such as food, water, shelter.

Maslow believed that if a need remained unsatisfied this would generate a motivation to act, and that basic needs (those at the lower levels) needed to be satisfied before higher ones could become motivating. For instance, we need to eat before we can set about making our environment secure or improving our self-esteem through work. The top end of the structure, at least, is dynamic. We may have a self-actualising need to teach competently, but once we have achieved this there are other aspects of our potential which we might seek to actualise.

> Theme link (**Humanistic theories of personality**)
>
> Humanistic theories concentrate on the whole self and reject the notion of reductionism in understanding humans. The approach is *phenomenological* which, in a crude definition, means that priority is given to whatever people experience, whether or not we would agree that their experience is actually valid. This has often been termed the 'third force' within mainstream psychology, intended to mean that it took a new direction away from both psychoanalysis and behaviourism. Rather than seeing humans as motivated internally by sinister unconscious forces or externally by mere physical 'reinforcements', humanism views humans as in control of their own actions and positively motivated. That is, in optimum circumstances people will choose to be positive towards others and towards their own direction of growth. It is only when people are pressed by circumstances, or when they do not listen to their own inner voice or use their own value system, that outcomes become negative and people become alienated, hate their work, turn to crime or turn away from a healthy attitude towards productive work.

One criticism of Maslow's model is that it has been hard to establish empirical evidence in support of this particular arrangement of needs and for the proposal that one must be satisfied before another. Betz (1982), using the theory, predicted that women staying at home should focus more on safety and social needs than would professional working women. However, both these groups rated self-actualisation and autonomy relatively equally and overall the ranking of needs did not fit Maslow's proposed order. Further weaknesses of the theory are that it is difficult to predict when a particular level of need will be activated and that some behaviour can be directed at several kinds of need at once. One advantage of the theory has been its popularity with management and Rollinson *et al.*, (1998) argue that this has at least caused managers to pay attention to the higher needs of their subordinates.

Alderfer's system (1972) proposed just three categories of need: existence, relatedness and growth. Basically, **existence** includes physiological and safety needs, **relatedness** refers to social needs and **growth** incorporates self-esteem and actualisation needs. However the system proposed is *not* hierarchical and behaviour can be geared towards all categories at once. For example, a motivation for promotion will produce, if successful, extra cash for physical needs, a different perhaps more desirable set of work colleagues and greater opportunity for personal satisfaction and esteem. This model has also proved difficult to test empirically, but it is intuitively easier to grasp and a lot simpler to apply.

NEED FOR ACHIEVEMENT (NACH)

McClelland (1961) suggested that one's **Need for Achievement** (NAch) was of vital importance in the organisational setting. This is assumed to be an acquired, not innate, personality dimension on which we all can be rated. People high in NAch are highly motivated to succeed and like to perform moderately difficult tasks to a standard of excellence. In other words, NAch high scorers are those sometimes annoying people who always do things well, as does the character Hermione in the popular Harry Potter books.

It is a markedly Western phenomenon that society values *individual* achievement, competition and success. In *collectivist* societies (see Triandis, 1994) where group success and collective decision-making are often more important, a high NAch score might indicate a problematic person in a work situation.

reinforcement

The simple behaviourist view of motivation is that we do not need to assume such a concept to explain human behaviour since we cannot ever observe it directly. What we observe is that people work harder for some rewards (more technically 'reinforcements') and less for others. To invent a construct of 'motivation' adds nothing to the explanation of human behaviour.

EXPECTANCY THEORIES

Expectancy theories are strongly related to the principles of cognitive psychology. People are considered to be logical and rational in their approach to work and to make precise cognitive assessments of expected rewards for work before they take action. According to the original model (Vroom, 1964), motivation is a product of:

**Expectancy** – beliefs about one's ability to perform well.
**Instrumentality** – beliefs about likely outcomes (rewards) if one does perform well.
**Valence** – the value placed by the individual on those outcomes (rewards).

For instance, consider a childcare employee who is being appraised and invited to consider taking responsibility for reading materials for all 3–4 year olds in the nursery. The model predicts that she would be motivated to take on this task according to the multiplication of the three factors shown in the box.

As motivation is assumed to be a product of the factors E, I and V, if any value were zero then there would be no motivation at all, for instance if there is no reward. It is even possible that an employee could be de-motivated if one of the values were negative. I recall a manager who used to 'reward' good effort with further responsibilities, assuming that all employees were eager to do better

| Expectancy | | Instrumentality | | Valence |
|---|---|---|---|---|
| *Will I perform competently?* | | *Will there be rewards?* | | *How do I value those possible rewards?* |
| Do I know enough about appropriate books? Will I have time to complete the ordering, reorganise the shelves, etc? | X | Will I get a performance award? Will this count towards promotion? Will it look good on my CV? | X | Would the award be worth all that effort or just too small? Do I really want the hard work that goes with promotion? |

and bigger things (but for no tangible reward or recognition). Not surprisingly, employees did not rush to take on new roles or to show great enthusiasm, possibly because the valence of the rewards was negative! Leon (1981) showed that, where negative valence is involved, the theory does not work.

Like most other theories of motivation, research studies only partially support the model. Schwab *et al.* (1979) argue that measures of 'expectancy' do not predict performance very well and that multiplying E x I x V is probably not the most effective mathematical formula. However, Ilgen and Klein (1989) argue that, after the development of better measures of expectancies during the 1980s, expectancy theory can fairly accurately predict a person's work level and satisfaction. Landy (1985) argues that the theory at least prompts managers to pay attention to the perceptions of employees about their potential for performing a task effectively (do I have the skills? do I have adequate resources?) and also to the kinds of reward employees value – it is no use offering a promotion with little increase in salary.

Expectancy theory has been applied in the United States where companies offered employees what became known as 'cafeteria compensation'. Here employees are permitted to choose from among several alternatives those rewards that have the highest valence for them. For instance, apart from basic salary, employees could top up their overall package with different kinds of insurance for themselves or their dependants, extra leave days and so on.

EQUITY THEORY

Equity theory is based largely on the views of Adams (1965) and concentrates on the comparison by an individual of two things:

- the balance of inputs to outputs: what I put into this job compared with what I get out of it.
- the comparison of my input/outcome balance with the balance of other workers.

In a general way, if you put a lot into a job and get little reward you will feel disgruntled. However this is all relative. If you see that your colleagues suffer in much the same way, you are not going to feel quite so bad about it, but if you work all hours under great stress for the same pay as someone who knocks off at five on the dot and never turns up when extra effort is needed, then you will feel that things are not equitable.

Equity is experienced when a person's input/output ratio is perceived as similar to other co-workers. For an individual, if outputs are greater than inputs then they are being over-rewarded. If others are not being similarly over-rewarded then **inequity motivation** should develop whereby the individual is motivated to restore equity. In this case they would eventually feel guilty and might take on tasks for others or suggest (in the extreme) a re-evaluation of their job. Early research (Adams and Rosenbaum, 1962) showed that students asked to perform a paid market research task, for which they were told they were seriously under-qualified, worked significantly harder than control students who were led to believe they were well qualified.

A much quicker and more energetic response would be expected where workers perceive themselves as relatively under-rewarded. This may well occur for a group of workers as a whole when management or executive members enjoy ever greater bonuses and pay increases, company cars and long lunches, while the lower workforce is under increasing stress, working long hours and always under threat of redundancy. This was pretty much the situation in many large companies in the UK during the late 1980s and up to the mid-1990s. Sometimes chief executives and managing directors receive enormous pay and bonus packages even when the company is struggling and share prices are plummeting, as happened in 2000–2001 in British Telecom. This will certainly result in perceptions of serious inequity.

Perceptions of inequity can shift as employees compare themselves with different reference groups. Before institutions of further and higher education were made independent during the 1980s, lecturers probably compared themselves mainly with those in other colleges and universities, and perhaps with others in 'caring' services. However, the shift to harsher working conditions and an emphasis on the financial basis of education has produced a change in reference. Lecturers are now beginning to require fees for previously free services and to compare themselves with more highly paid professionals such as lawyers or engineers (see Radford, 2000).

During the 1990s the focus within equity theory turned towards a broader perspective of general organisational justice. Equity theory, as described above, looked at people's perception of **distributive justice** – seeing how rewards are actually distributed. Arnold et al. (1998) argue that people also pay attention to **procedural justice** – whether the systems used in an organisation to distribute rewards are fair. The downsizing and de-layering that has been common in many companies during the 1990s has led some employees to feel that their *psychological contract* with the company has been broken and consequently they are less likely to take on voluntary tasks or feel loyalty to their employers (Parks and Kidder, 1994). On the other hand, perception of fair procedural justice within a company may cause an employee to feel loyalty even though they see themselves as poorly rewarded relative to others outside their organisation.

## GOAL-SETTING

This theory is acclaimed by Arnold *et al.* (1998) as 'probably the most consistently supported theory in work and organisational psychology' (p.258). Starting in the 1960s, Locke researched and refined the model over the decades, and in 1990 Locke and Latham were able to claim the following well supported principles:

**Difficult goals produce higher performance than easy ones** – so long as you want to do a job then the harder it is the more motivated you will be to complete it. Notice straight away the clash between this and expectancy theory where being *more* certain of success would predict higher motivation. Presumably with more difficult goals, even if accepted, there must be slightly *less* certainty of success. However, much practical research supports the more difficult goals = more motivation formula (see Locke and Latham, 1990; Rodgers and Hunter, 1991).

**Specific goals are more effective than general 'do your best' goals** – this is probably *the* most important principle of the theory. Imagine that your tutor tells you simply to 'do your best' to improve in class next term. A more structured and successful approach would be to set you certain targets: improve attendance from 70 to 80 per cent; submit an essay plan for comment two weeks before it is due in; complete draft writing of the essay one week before it is due, and so on.

Where people have been set possible difficult and specific goals Locke's theory has been supported in 90 per cent of laboratory and field research studies, a phenomenal figure compared with most other organisational psychology theories.

**Knowledge of results** – finding out how you are doing on each specific goal is important in improving performance, particularly where the result is the setting of a somewhat higher goal. For instance, hearing that you are selling above your monthly target is not likely to motivate stronger performance, but the information that you are slightly *behind* target is likely to result in a revised higher goal for the coming month.

**Participation** – most contemporary appraisal systems assume that people are better motivated if they participate in the setting of their own goals. However, Locke concluded (1981) that participation had no effect and that people are equally motivated if goals are simply handed to them. This debate about participation led to a classic series of experiments by Locke and Erez, the latter's research apparently showing that participation in goal-setting *did* work. The crucial difference that emerged between the two researchers' work was that in Erez's studies, those who were not participating in goal-setting were simply given their goals whereas Locke's non-participators were also given encouragement to believe they could achieve their goals. (Latham, Erez and Locke, 1988).

The application of this last finding is very important. In many work situations it is just not feasible to have all workers participate in the setting of complex goals. However, managers learning from this research can take note that goals need to be realistic in order for employees to then 'own' these goals and work more effectively towards them.

One critique of goal-setting theory could be that much work, including that described just above, has been carried out in the laboratory. However, much supportive evidence has also come from studies in work settings and Locke *et al*. (1981) reported that the average improvement in performance in field studies was 16 per cent. The work settings themselves have not all been 'soft' ones but have included both logging and haulage companies.

Problems in real work goal-setting include the issue of conflicting goals. Teachers, for instance, cannot work effectively under the competing goals of both producing better exam results *and* reducing the costs of their teaching or working longer hours. A further unresolved issue is that most studies have measured performance in terms of *quantity*; it is not clear that *quality* is also improved through goal-setting. It has however been shown in the UK that goal-setting strategies have lowered accident rates and improved industrial health and safety behaviour (Cooper *et al.*, 1994).

**Goal-setting and individual differences** – Naturally we would not expect goal-setting to work the same way on all people. Hollenbeck *et al*. (1989) found that people with a high need for achievement and with an internal locus of control were more likely to be committed to difficult goals after a goal-setting experience. This was particularly so where people participated in the goal-setting process. Since goal-setting is a cognitive theory it is also likely that different cognitive styles, especially those associated with planning and strategies, will have an impact on how goal-setting works.

Work motivation theories can be based on needs (Maslow, Alderfer, McClelland), on the processes of reinforcement, on the cognitive processes of expectancy and equity, and on the procedure of goal-setting. Each has strengths and weaknesses and some look at different aspects of the work situation. Some, such as Maslow's, are rather vaguely defined but popular with management for their lofty and/or practical ideas, whereas others, such as Locke's in particular, are clearly defined and have impressive supporting empirical evidence.

# Improving motivation

Having reviewed several major theories of motivation we should now be in a position to review how each one answers the two following questions:

- What is the relationship between motivation and work performance?
- How can we improve motivation?

In the table below answers to these questions are outlined for each model we have covered so far. We will continue with the topic of motivation and performance in the next section.

• **Table G.1:** The relationship between motivation theories and performance and the improvement of motivation

| Theory | Relationship | Improving motivation |
|--------|-------------|---------------------|
| Maslow's hierarchy of needs | No clear empirical relationship established between satisfaction of needs at one level and consequent effects on performance. | Match workers' rewards to their position in the hierarchy. Alter rewards as people move up the hierarchy. At least, recognise that people have a variety of different needs to satisfy – what satisfies one may not satisfy another. |
| Alderfer's | No clear empirical relationship between greater satisfaction of needs and consequent effects on performance. | Ensure that needs are directed as far as possible to all three categories of need: existence, relatedness and growth. |

| NAch | Predicts behaviour which is ambitious, conscientious, responsibility- and opportunity-seeking. People high on NAch produce more than they consume – see Furnham, 1997, p.207. | NAch cannot be easily increased in adults but achievement theorists stress the long-term importance of parental expectations, supportive and stimulating upbringing, encouraging adventurousness in children, educational stimuli and so on. |
| --- | --- | --- |
| Expectancy theory | E x I x V was supposed to estimate motivation and thence performance. Weak support from early work but later, with E x I x V modified, fairly good prediction of work level. | Ensure: People are given goals which they believe they can achieve. Rewards are clearly associated with good performance. Rewards are those that employees value. |
| Equity theory | Early laboratory studies suggest 'inequity motivation' does affect performance; later work supports idea that perceived procedural justice maintains performance but that perceived distributive or procedural injustice lowers it. | Ensure that employees perceive equity by making comparisons clear and rationalising these. Also ensure that employees do not make inappropriate comparisons within or between organisations. |
| Goal-setting theory | Very clear evidence of effectiveness, as much as 16 per cent increase in performance in real work settings and 90 per cent support across all studies. | Set clear, achievable and specific goals with one's employees or at least with strong encouragement (if goals are set for employees). Give appropriate and useful feedback on performance at regular intervals. |

**Section summary**   The various theories covered in the first section all carry implications for improving motivation at work. Table 6.1 outlines these and also indicates the relationship between motivation and performance implicit in each theory. There are further implications for performance and motivation improvement contained in the two major theories in the next section.

# Motivation and performance

Although we have also covered the relationship between motivation and performance in Table 6.1 above, there are two approaches to motivation which are worth outlining in detail. The reader should note that these two models also carry implications for improving performance though in rather general terms.

## HERZBERG'S HYGIENE THEORY

Herzberg's (1966) 'two-factor theory' proposed that motivation to work was not caused primarily by external incentives such as pay and conditions. True positive motivation came from the job itself, the feeling of doing something worthwhile. If certain hygiene factors were missing we would feel dissatisfaction, and motivation might well be threatened, but to *increase* motivation one needed to ensure that certain 'motivators' were present. Only these could lead to the *presence of satisfaction* rather than the *absence of dissatisfaction*. Herzberg was scornful of incentive schemes and advised the manipulation of true motivators to get total (internal) worker commitment – see Hollway, 1991, p.103.

**Hygiene factors** include pay, conditions of employment, company policy, administration, supervision system, security and so on. These are **extrinsic** factors because they are outside of the job itself.

**Motivators** are **intrinsic** to the job and include recognition, challenge, perfection of skills and so on. These factors produce job satisfaction if present. According to Herzberg, one was not dissatisfied without them but just not satisfied!

Note that pay is usually considered a 'hygiene' factor in this system and hence not particularly motivating unless low. Certainly at high levels, pay becomes somewhat irrelevant to motivation. Highly-paid sports people, who can earn many thousands if not millions even for losing, must be motivated more by factors other than money, such as status and success. However, there are occasions where, in ordinary jobs, higher pay is a 'motivator'. This occurs even where the pay difference is small but receiving that difference is a sign or recognition of one's achieved status in the job and one's superiority over others.

Herzberg *et al.* questioned 200 engineers and accountants. These are professional occupations where the job holders have advanced qualifications and will have worked hard to achieve their position. They are the sort of people who, irrespective of the particular job they may find themselves in, pay a lot of attention to intrinsic job satisfaction. Pay will not be the sole most important factor for them when they assess the quality of their employment. We might find, if we question employees in unstimulating and repetitive jobs, that pay becomes much more of a motivator and satisfaction in one's work might not figure high on these workers' agenda at all.

The problem here is then that the sample might have been particularly narrow and therefore biased. The effect found might have been limited only to the type of population from which the samples were drawn.

## THE JOB CHARACTERISTICS MODEL (JCM)

Hackman and Oldham's (1976) job characteristics theory was influenced by Herzberg's model and also by expectancy theory (p.86). The model is outlined in Figure 6.1. They held that job satisfaction, motivation, work quality and performance are influenced indirectly by five core job dimensions which are:

- **Skill variety:** the variety of skills and abilities required by a job.
- **Task identity:** the extent to which the employee witnesses the completion of an entire piece of work (e.g. cooking a whole pizza rather than just adding pepperoni).
- **Task significance:** the extent to which a job has impact on others within or outside the organisation; for instance a teacher is aware of their student's exam results and consequent effects on students' lives; a bricklayer usually does not meet the people who will use the building and may not even see the final completed structure.

These first three dimensions influence one 'critical psychological state' – the **experienced meaningfulness of work**.

- **Autonomy:** the extent of the employee's freedom to design and structure their job influences experience of responsibility for one's work.
- **Feedback:** the degree to which the job itself can provide information to employees on how well they are doing the job gives them knowledge of results about their work progress.

The three critical psychological states in turn influence several major aspects of work behaviour and experience, as shown on the right-hand side of Figure 6.1.

Hackman and Oldham developed the Job Diagnostic Survey (JDS) to measure all the variables depicted in Figure 6.1 and produced a formula to measure Motivating Potential Score (MPS) as follows:

$$MPS = \frac{SV + TI + TS}{3} \times AU \times FB$$

Note that without any autonomy (AU) or feedback (FB) the MPS score becomes zero, no matter how great the skill variety, task interest or task significance. This is probably a little too pessimistic. Other criticisms of the model have been that: the model does not work well for people who are low in growth-need strength, a concept based on Maslow's notions of need for self-esteem and actualisation; most studies have simply correlated

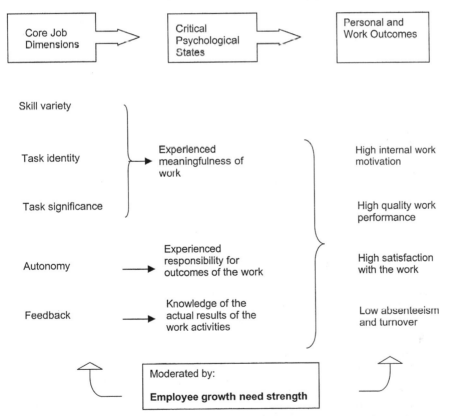

• **Figure 6.1:** Hackman and Oldham's (1980) *Job Characteristics Model of Working Motivation.* Adapted from J.R. Hackman and G.R. Oldham (1980) *Work Redesign:* Addison-Wesley Publishing Co, Inc.

characteristics with outcomes. They have not evaluated whether changes in job characteristics lead to better performance or greater job satisfaction (see job redesign in Chapter 7). However, Arnold *et al.* (1988) say that 'the JCM [model] has stood the empirical test reasonably well, especially considering the relatively large number of connections between specific variables it proposes' (p.464).

**Section summary**    Herzberg's theory identifies both external factors (pay, conditions) and internal factors (satisfaction, fulfilment) involved in motivation to work. It helped to focus attention in organisational research and practice on what motivates people about their actual job, rather than focusing only on material factors as in Taylorism. It has been extremely influential and helped produce several models including the more recently influential model of Hackman and Oldham – the Job Characteristics Model. This relates more specific Job Characteristics to psychological states and, in turn, to various work outcomes including motivation, satisfaction and performance.

## KEY TERMS

autonomy (JCM)
distributive justice
equity theory
esteem needs (Maslow)
existence (Alderfer)
expectancy theory
experienced meaningfulness of work (JCM)
extrinsic motivation
feedback
goal setting
growth (Alderfer)
Herzberg's 'hygiene' theory
hierarchy of needs (Maslow)
humanistic theories
hygiene factors (Herzberg)
inequity motivation (equity theory)
Instrumentality (expectancy theory)
intrinsic motivation
job characteristics model (JCM)
knowledge of results
motivators (Herzberg)

**NAch**
**physiological needs (Maslow)**
**procedural justice**
**reinforcement**
**relatedness (Alderfer)**
**safety needs (Maslow)**
**self-actualisation needs (Maslow)**
**social needs (Maslow)**
**valence (expectancy theory)**
**skill variety (JCM)**
**task identity (JCM)**
**task significance (JCM)**

## EXERCISE 1

List the intrinsic and extrinsic factors of motivation associated with being a student. Compare these with those of a colleague if possible.

## EXERCISE 2

Mr Grindham is the managing director of Grimtown Bearings and Pistons. This year he is going for the South-Western Institute of Nasty Employers' (SWINE) Golden Rock-Bottom Morale award. To achieve this he must produce the most alienated, disaffected, complaining and de-motivated workforce in the area. Help him to win this award by listing all the features he should introduce into his organisation (if not already there) in order to produce this workforce. Follow this by producing a consultancy project designed to improve motivation to the highest level possible – in your view anyway.

## ESSAY QUESTIONS

1. Critically evaluate at least two theories of work motivation.

2. How can worker motivation be improved? Provide answers with reference to several theories of worker motivation and to research studies where possible.

# Further reading

Furnham, A. (1997) *The  Psychology of Behaviour at Work*. Hove: Psychology
Press. Chapter 6 (Work motivation and satisfaction).
Hollway, W. (1991) *Work Psychology and Organizational Behaviour.* London:
Sage. Chapter 6 (Motivating employees).

# Websites

http://www.cba.uri.edu/Scholl/Papers/Self_Concept_Motivation.HTM
Long and sometimes complex article on self-concept and work motivation.
Tries to integrate all models into a comprehensive review of the interaction
between management motivating systems and personal, internal
motivation factors. Worth a read.

http://bized.ac.uk/stafsup/options/work/motivtut.htm
Bixed's site on motivation – Tutor notes.

http://bized.ac.uk:8080/stafsup/options/work/motiv.htm
Bized's site on motivation – Student notes.

http://www.ee.uwa.edu.au/~ccroft/em333/lecl.html
Useful points on most of the topics in this chapter from University of West
Australia.

# seven

# Quality of working life

## Introduction

In the early years of the 20th century when principles of psychology were first applied to the work situation, F.W. Taylor introduced some extreme ideas into the debate about the best ways to improve production and eliminate inefficiency at work. The principles of what became known as 'Taylorism' (or 'scientific management') are probably familiar to you and although most managers today will express something very close to horror at the sheer inhumanity of the ideas, many production organisations operate in a way not so different from what was then recommended. Taylorism holds that:

- Jobs should be studied scientifically and broken down into the simplest set of tasks
- Specified instructions should be given for each task along with a (previously measured) time for completion
- Workers should be given these instructions and should take no part in decisions about how they work and what they do
- Workers should only be rewarded with money.

The clearly implied management position is that no worker really wants to help the organisation, or to derive satisfaction from work; workers merely want to take home a pay packet to buy material satisfaction.

The effect of Taylorism in the UK was not as marked as in the USA, largely because of the prior existence of relatively powerful Trades Unions (Hollway, 1991). Nevertheless, production line factories have generally worked in this way and the effects of this kind of working have led to consideration of several themes:

- Does repetitive and mindless work produce stress?
- Is it important to measure and allow for job satisfaction?
- What can be done to improve job satisfaction and the general quality of working life?

These are the topics for each section in this chapter.

# Work stress – causes and effects

People use the term 'stress' in several ways. A common use is to refer to the feelings and reactions within a person when things 'get too much'. Selye (1946) attempted to explain stress-related illnesses using a model he called the **general adaptation syndrome** – a set of stages through which an individual passes when stressful conditions overpower them. There are three stages to the syndrome. **Alarm reaction:** the individual lowers resistance then summons energy to produce defence mechanisms against the increased external pressure. **Resistance:** if this stage is successful the individual adapts to the increased

• **Table 7.1:** Stress-related symptoms and illnesses. *Main source:* Arnold *et al.* (1998)

| Physical symptoms | Illnesses caused or worsened |
|---|---|
| Insomnia, excessive or constant tiredness | Depression |
| Constipation, diarrhoea, irritable bowels | Hypertension |
| High blood pressure | Diabetes |
| Loss of appetite | Heart diseases |
| Fainting | Migraine |
| Twitches, tics, fidgeting | Asthma |
| Impotence | Ulcers |
| | Colitis |
| **Behavioural or psychological symptoms** | Arthritis |
| | Skin disorders |
| Irritability, anger (actual or suppressed) | Tuberculosis |
| Lack of verve, interest in life | Hayfever |
| Feeling a failure, ugly, unwanted, bad, incompetent, paranoid, neglected, alone | Chronic indigestion |
| Agoraphobia, claustrophobia, hypochondria | |
| Being/feeling unable to cope with normal pressures of life | |
| Forgetfulness, indecisiveness | |

pressure and their bodily systems return to equilibrium level; if unsuccessful they move on to the third stage. **Exhaustion:** adaptive mechanisms fail or collapse and the individual usually exhibits symptoms of illness.

Later theories defined stress as the external pressures impinging on an individual. Others saw stress as an *interaction*. Cummings and Cooper (1979), for instance, saw the stress process as a misfit between the individual and the environmental pressures they experience. An individual generally contains their physical and psychological processes within a 'range of stability' (a steady state). Any environmental occurrence can become a 'stressor'. The *interpretation* is all-important. Where I might feel energised at the prospect of running a special conference, your reaction to this new responsibility might be the onset of a stress-related illness. Table 7.1 lists some common symptoms of stress and illnesses that can be initiated or worsened by stress.

EFFECTS OF STRESS ON PERFORMANCE

We mustn't assume that all stress is bad. A moment's thought will tell us that a certain degree of stress can be highly motivating. The computer game Tetris involves stressful frustration, yet it is just this factor which makes it obsessively motivating for many players. Athletes require a certain amount of competitive stress in order to perform at their best. A dull job with no obvious stress can, paradoxically, become stressful simply through its relentless monotony.

Figure 7.1 illustrates the well researched relationship between **arousal** and performance. If we are over-aroused ('pressured') our performance deteriorates, as does our quality of life and possibly our motivation to do well. On the other hand, too little stimulation leading to boredom and apathy, has a lowering effect on performance and will also reduce quality and probably motivation too.

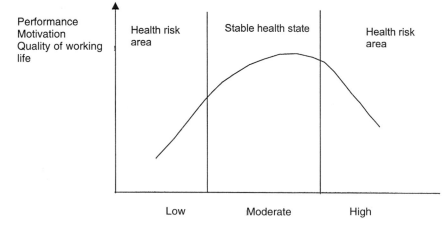

• **Figure 7.1:** Relationship between arousal (stress), performance and health. Based partly on Melhuish, 1978 (Arnold)

• **Table 7.2:** Possible sources of stress at work

| General source | Examples | Comment |
|---|---|---|
| **Factors intrinsic to the job** | Working conditions<br>Shift work<br>Long hours<br>Risk and danger<br>New technology<br>Work overload<br>Work underload<br>Physical, psychological and temporal conditions | See Chapter 8<br><br>Especially computerised work<br><br>Too little to do; boring unstimulating work<br><br>See Chapter 8 |
| **Role in the organisation** | Role ambiguity | Particularly in a new position there may be a lack of clarity about what one is supposed to do, what authority and responsibility one has, what exactly is expected. |
| | Role conflict | A supervisor may feel conflict if also a union representative. |
| | Personality variables | These will interact with the former two factors. Some people have a lower tolerance of ambiguity; anxious individuals may experience greater stress in any conflict situation. |
| | Responsibility | Responsibility for people can be more stressful than responsibility for things (e.g. the budget, buildings) partly because there are often unpleasant decisions to be made about colleagues' lives and positions. |
| **Relationships at work** | With superiors | For example, 'considerate' superiors appear to produce less stress. Stress can be experienced where a superior gives unhelpful criticism and uses authority without justification. |
| | With subordinates | Difficulties with maintaining respect and co-operation or with delegation of tasks, may cause stress. |
| | With colleagues | Co-operation and mutual support can reduce stress – see the studies in socio-technical systems p.106. |
| **Career development** | Job security<br>Retirement<br>Job performance | These factors include the stress caused by the threat of losing or leaving work or from evaluation or appraisal. |
| **Organisational structure and climate** | | One can feel detached and isolated from an organisation or one can feel one belongs. Participation in decision-making can increase job satisfaction and therefore ease strain for the employee. |

## SOURCES OF STRESS AT WORK

It would be an interesting exercise for you to try and list now all the factors to do with being at work that could contribute to increasing perceived and actual stress. Having done this, look at Table 7.2 which contains a list of headings from Arnold *et al.* (1998, p.430) which cites research evidence to support each factor as a significant source of stress.

**Type A and Type B personalities** were identified by Friedman and Rosenman (1974). Type As were described as impatient, ambitious, driven, hard-working and competitive. Type Bs could be equally ambitious but not in such a driven and frenetic manner. Early research associated Type As with increased risk of heart disease and other typical stress-related diseases. However, Ganster *et al.* (1991) reviewed the validity of the Type A concept and suggested that the relationship might be far more complex, with Type A personality being only a factor (and probably not such a unitary one) that combines with other personality characteristics to increase health risk.

**Burnout** appeared as a concept in the 1980s to account for the withdrawal of people in certain professions from the frontline of their work. It was thought that this occurred through excessive demands which resulted in the worker first suffering emotional exhaustion, then developing a more detached attitude to work and the people in it, and finally experiencing a sense of frustration and feelings of low personal achievement. The phenomenon was found (in the USA) to be particularly associated with the caring service professions, for instance, nurses (Leiter and Maslach, 1988), teachers (Byrne, 1993) and social workers (Wright and Cropanzano, 1998).

> **Section summary**
>
> Stress is variously interpreted as internal feelings of pressure, environmental inputs and demands or an *interaction* between inputs and each individual's interpretations of these as demands. Behavioural and psychological symptoms of stress are listed. Stress can be interpreted as an arousing factor and, as such, can weaken performance when it is either too weak or too strong. Sources of stress can arise from the job itself or from relationships with others at work and the organisation in general. Type A has been identified as a personality type associated with stress related disease. 'Burnout' can result from extreme stress at work.

# Job satisfaction

If a job involves too much stress, or too little stimulation, we might expect it to produce less satisfaction, other things being equal, than a moderately stressful job. For example, workers in repetitive machine-paced jobs, with no control over rate and pace of work, experience great stress and have high levels of adrenalin, anxiety, depression and somatic (bodily) complaints (Smith, 1985).

Part of the reaction to Taylorism by work and organisational psychologists involved theories and research which saw job satisfaction as a crucial variable affecting efficiency and productivity. **Job satisfaction** refers to the ways people feel about their organisation, the people they work with and the physical conditions and rewards of their job, but especially intrinsic rewards, such as feeling good about what you do, enjoying it, feeling it is worthwhile. These factors were thought quite irrelevant by Taylorism.

Theme link – Methodology (**Psychological measurement scales**)

Psychologists use many measurement scales to assess psychological characteristics. Very often these use what is known as a Likert type response format. Given a particular statement, e.g. 'My work is satisfying', you are asked to choose the answer closest to your own honest reaction from: 'strongly agree, agree, neutral/undecided, disagree, strongly disagree'. Note that each item is a statement not a question so the term 'scale' is used in preference to the term 'questionnaire'.

Each item response is given a score from 1 ('strongly agree') to 5 ('strongly disagree'). Hence, if you 'agree' with item 2 below you will receive a score of two. However if you agree with item 1 you would also receive a score of two, yet this item shows dissatisfaction whereas item 2 showed satisfaction. Hence, in order for satisfied respondents overall to receive a high score, items like item 2 would be reversed – you would receive a score of four, not two (five would become one and so on). Items should express both positive and negative attitudes, otherwise there might be a tendency simply to carry on agreeing or disagreeing with items that all run in the same direction. This responding tendency is known as *response* set. The reason that scales use several, rather just one item, is that researchers want their measures to be reliable. Each item is an estimate of the variable being measured, e.g. 'satisfaction with co-workers'. The more items, the more accurate the estimate; the closer the measures on each item then the more consistent the set of items is and hence the scale is said to have good *reliability*. Whether or not the scale in fact measures what was intended (e.g. job satisfaction) however, is a different matter – one of *validity*.

Examples of possible items from a scale measuring job satisfaction:
1. I find my work generally boring
2. My work is stimulating

## MEASURING JOB SATISFACTION

Hackman and Oldham (1975) produced the **Job Diagnostic Survey** (JDS) which uses a variety of items to measure the various components of the Job Characteristics Model (JCM – see Chapter 6). This included a measure of job satisfaction as one of the major 'outcomes' of the model. Loher *et al.* (1985) found that the correlation between job characteristics and job satisfaction was 0.68 for people high in growth-need strength, but only 0.38 for those low in growth-need strength.

Other researchers have developed scales specifically to measure job satisfaction. An early approach was that of Kunin (1955) who asked workers to choose the face, from a varied set of expressions, that most closely resembled their feelings about their job. The problem with this scale is that it can only measure *global* satisfaction. We can't tell which *aspects* of a job (people, tasks, conditions) are more or less satisfying.

A very popular scale has been Smith, Kendal and Hulin's **Job Descriptive Index** (JDI) which asks respondents to agree or disagree that certain adjectives describe factors of their work. A limitation is that there are only five factors, four of these being extrinsic (pay, supervision, promotion, co-workers) and just one intrinsic factor (the nature of the work itself).

Theme link – Methodology (**Measurement bias and sampling**)

Some major criticisms of the JCM model emerged from a review of the research literature by Roberts and Glick (1982). One of these criticisms was that almost all research results had been obtained via questionnaire. The problem here is that questionnaires rely on self-reports from respondents. Hence they are subject to several possible errors such as:

- Respondents might not view their behaviour as objectively as do independent observers
- Not all respondents will interpret a question or statement in the same way
- Respondents will not disclose behaviour which is embarrassing to them or regarded as anti-social or immoral
- Respondents may therefore be subject to **social desirability** factors – the tendency to answer according to current social norms rather than report how they actually behave.

Many researchers make use of **triangulation** – they use several different methods to assess behaviour, attitudes or performance, each taken from a different perspective (for instance, questionnaire, interview, observation). Of interest here is the disparity between, say, an employee's view of their performance and that of their colleagues and supervisors.

The **Index of Organisational Reactions** (IOR) (Smith, 1976) is a far more comprehensive 42-item scale using several items, all scored from 1 to 5 under each of the following headings: *supervision, company identification, kind of work, amount of work, co-workers, physical work conditions, financial rewards, career future*. This still concentrates heavily on extrinsic factors.

**Section summary**   Job satisfaction refers to the satisfaction people derive from their work, especially emphasising *intrinsic* factors of fulfilment. Several measures have been developed (including the JDS, JDI and IOR). Such measures are examples of psychological measurement scales and these need to be both reliable and valid in addition to avoiding various sources of measurement bias including response set, sampling and social desirability factors.

# Increasing job satisfaction

Organisational psychologists became worried about the effects of Taylorism in the early to mid-1900s, or at least about the ways in which work had become automated, mindless and lacking in personal involvement, responsibility or stimulation. Even by 1913 it was noted in the USA at Ford, where new assembly line factories had reduced jobs to very highly specialised routines, that turnover was costing the company more than two million dollars a year (Hollway, 1991). By the 1950s job design had become an economic necessity since there was near full employment and therefore workers could choose not to take boring jobs. As a reaction to the sheer dehumanising aspects of repetitive work, there arose a movement of researchers who promoted what they called the **quality of working life**. This movement drew significantly on the work of Herzberg which we discussed in Chapter 6, and on the tradition known as **socio-technical systems**. Both these approaches emphasised the need to design jobs with people in mind, not bare efficiency.

## JOB REDESIGN

The issues came to be discussed as **job redesign** and **job enrichment**. This referred to changing the nature of jobs to make them more intrinsically rewarding and it was generally assumed that this would lead to greater satisfaction and improved production and efficiency. Herzberg's 'hygiene' theory (p.92) was influential in promoting these ideas. Herzberg argued that pay and other 'hygiene' factors would only stave off *dissatisfaction*. Extra rewards (e.g. bonuses) only work in the short term, and so to get more productivity the incentive must be offered again. On the other hand *satisfaction* came from intrinsic motivators, the kind of incentives which do not need re-introduction. Work is rewarding in itself if structured correctly. Miner (1992, p.87) lists eight features of Herzberg's later 'orthodox job enrichment' approach which sought to give jobs this motivating structure, listed in the box below.

| Direct feedback | Non-evaluative feedback on work performance goes straight to the employee, not through a superior. |
|---|---|
| Client relationships | College technicians might be brought to see tutors as their 'customers' or 'clients'; teachers to see their students also as 'customers'. |
| New learning | Employees are given opportunities to learn new and meaningful skills. |
| Scheduling | Employees are permitted to organise their own work patterns within reasonable limits and deadlines (e.g. 'flexitime'; working at home). |
| Unique expertise | Using one's special skills and knowledge; e.g. being permitted to bake an apple pie to one's own recipe rather than following a given formula. |
| Control over resources | Having an individual budget for which one is responsible. |
| Direct communications authority | Being able to communicate as necessary to get the job done. For instance, communicating with seniors outside one's group without having to go through one's own senior. |
| Personal accountability | The employee is directly accountable for their work. |

The JCM approach to work motivation also has implications for job redesign, though few studies have actually tackled the question of whether changing characteristics does have an effect on motivation and thence satisfaction. The model does not offer much advice on how to change job characteristics and, in particular, we know that there are problems where workers are low in growth-need strength.

**Socio-technical systems** theory was based in a psycho-analytic tradition and stressed that there was an inseparable *interaction* between the technical systems that are introduced at work and the ways in which people engage with them and with each other. De Board (1978) stated that the technical and social components at work:

> ... are interlinked with each other and changes in one will automatically lead to changes in the other. The whole system can now be perceived as a 'socio-technical' system and its total effectiveness will depend on the balance achieved between the social and the technological components. (p.96)

An example of the way in which a new technical system can drastically alter the ways in which people interact and communicate is given below.

**Goodbye gossip – hello flame mail**

A good modern example of the socio-technical systems philosophy is the introduction of e-mail to offices. Prior to e-mail people used to chat about issues in corridors, offices or the staff room. More serious concerns were addressed using a hard copy memo. Nowadays, e-mailing has to some extent replaced informal live chats. Instead, an e-mail is fired off and responded to without the correspondents ever meeting one another. People meet in the corridor and suddenly remember that they've had a complex interchange with someone whom they're now facing. Very often it becomes clear that chatting about the issue 'live' is a good deal more efficient and simple than tapping away at the keyboard.

More seriously, it is all too easy to respond abruptly to some issue by e-mail and to find a series of flame mail messages developing to the point where there are serious interpersonal problems, again without those involved ever having met face to face.

This is a modern example of an interaction between a technical system (e-mail) and the consequent changes occurring in the pattern of social relationships among those who start to use it.

Trist and Bamforth developed these views partly as a result of their research study (1951) in the Durham coalfields. Here management had created serious industrial problems by introducing a new technology known as the Longwall method. Prior to this the miners had worked in small, self-managed and highly co-operative teams (usually of three), negotiating a price with management for their coal, and supporting one another's families when accidents occurred. The Longwall method involved fast cutting machines and made small teams superfluous. Groups were now 50 strong, existing social structures were disrupted and each group carried out just one major task per shift. Some groups now did jobs of lower status and all were supervised by one person, where before they had been self-regulating. The new technology, involving specialisation and close supervision, and intended to be more efficient, had produced problems of low satisfaction, higher absenteeism and lower productivity.

The researchers suggested that operation of the new technology should permit the inclusion of some of the earlier working practices. With a consideration of both social and technological factors, increased productivity and decreased absenteeism were among some of the outcomes.

## ENRICHING JOBS TO RAISE JOB SATISFACTION

Most job enrichment programmes seek to increase *variety* (types of task), *autonomy* (freedom to choose how to complete tasks and schedule work goals) or *completeness* (extent to which there is an end result that the employee can witness) (Wall, 1982).

There are several ways to change jobs and these include **job enlargement:** this can be vertical (additional responsibilities, more complex tasks) or horizontal (additional tasks at the same current level), and **job rotation**: employees swap tasks or jobs at regular frequent intervals.

Vertical enlargement can occur at the level of the small group in which case it is known as a **semi-autonomous work group**. Here, a small group is given broader responsibility and organises its own ways of accomplishing its tasks. This was introduced some time ago in Volvo's plants in Sweden and is now quite common in several UK car factories.

| Sources of increased job satisfaction | |
|---|---|
| Leadership research | In Chapter 5 we saw that a democratic leadership style appears to produce more satisfied (though not necessarily more productive) group members. This is in line with the findings on worker participation and responsibility discussed in this chapter and the last. We also saw that transformational leaders and those high in 'consideration' tend to produce more satisfied group members. |
| Group participation and communication | Continuing the participation theme we saw that people in less centralised, more communicative networks found their problem-solving tasks more satisfying. |
| Group conflict | Workers appear to be more satisfied where potential conflict is managed through discussion and open communication rather than by authoritarian measures. |
| Equity theory | The avoidance of *inequity motivation* should predict a higher level of overall satisfaction with the outcomes of one's job (p.88). Agho, Mueller & Price (1993) found that perceptions of *distributive justice* predicted job satisfaction. |
| Goal-setting | Although little research makes the connection, one would assume that people who are more productive at setting clear and harder goals also derive more satisfaction from their success. |

A problem with some of these programmes however is that workers can justifiably become suspicious of motives. Even where programmes are introduced with the genuine humanistic aim of increasing worker satisfaction (perhaps in tandem with the hoped-for increase in productivity), any increase in tasks or added responsibility can seem like sheer extra work and an increased potential for making bad decisions for which one is then accountable. One is reminded of the author's one-time 'rewarding' manager mentioned on p.86. This is why most programmes also seek, through discussion and group work, to raise awareness of the benefits of enriched jobs so that the new tasks and responsibilities are 'owned' by employees.

## IMPROVING THE QUALITY OF WORKING LIFE

We have seen that organisational psychologists can attempt to increase the quality of working life (QWL) through interventions that try to increase job satisfaction and reduce the ill-effects of repetitive and meaningless jobs. In addition, QWL can be enhanced through the reduction of work stress. This can be achieved in several ways, the most thorough-going of which is to change the stress source – that is to redesign the job in order to remove some of its inherent stress. This however is rarely done (Cooper and Cartwright, 1994) and most workplace interventions are aimed not at *removing* causes of stress, but at helping the individual employee to *cope* with it. These employment assistance programmes (EAPs) are discussed a little further at the end of Chapter 8.

QWL proponents argue that although organisations may find it costly to provide such support programmes, and particularly to remove workplace stress at source, it is even more costly *not* to maintain a high quality work environment. In order to count the costs an employer would need to measure absenteeism, accident rates, cost of recruitment, training of new staff and also such 'invisible' costs as job satisfaction, staff morale, the effects these have on client/customer relations and the organisation's overall image and status. In the next and final chapter we shall consider more factors to be considered when attempting to improve the quality of working life.

**Section summary**    Both the quality of working life and socio-technical systems movements sought to improve job design in the interests of creating greater autonomy and meaningfulness of work for employees. Herzberg distinguished between 'hygiene factors' and 'motivators', the latter providing job satisfaction. Socio-technical systems theory saw technology and social relationships as intimately related. Features of job enrichment include enlargement and rotation. QWL can also be improved though organisational strategies to reduce stress and promote healthy lifestyles at work.

# KEY TERMS

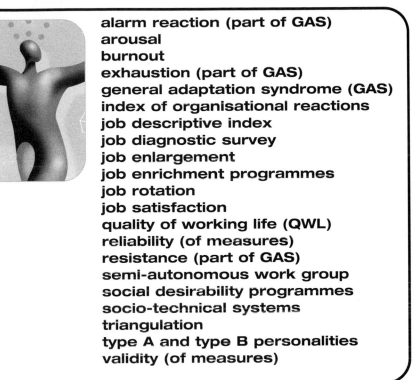

alarm reaction (part of GAS)
arousal
burnout
exhaustion (part of GAS)
general adaptation syndrome (GAS)
index of organisational reactions
job descriptive index
job diagnostic survey
job enlargement
job enrichment programmes
job rotation
job satisfaction
quality of working life (QWL)
reliability (of measures)
resistance (part of GAS)
semi-autonomous work group
social desirability programmes
socio-technical systems
triangulation
type A and type B personalities
validity (of measures)

## EXERCISE 1

First, list all the sources of stress that might occur in the jobs of:

• A school secretary
• A teacher or college lecturer
• A fast-food counter assistant
• A self-employed plumber.

In each case categorise the sources into short-term and relatively permanent. Then discuss how the short-term ones could be anticipated and better prepared for and how the permanent ones could be generally lessened. Now find out through group discussion how many of these sources actually have been tackled, and by what means, in real circumstances.

## EXERCISE 2

In a group first state two or three jobs that would suit you, including your present one if appropriate. For each, outline the sources of satisfaction that it would provide for you. Now decide which of these sources are internal (e.g. pride in the work) and which are external (salary, right kind of people to meet). Discuss, for each group member, which are the more important types of satisfaction to be obtained from a job and why.

## ESSAY QUESTIONS

1. What is meant by the 'quality of working life'? Discuss ways in which it can be improved at work.

2. Critically evaluate methods by which job satisfaction could be measured.

## Further reading

Cooper, C.L. *et al*. (1991) The impact of stress counselling at work. In P.L. Perrewe (Ed) Handbook of *Job Stress (Special Issue), Journal of Social Behaviour and Personality*, 6, 7, 411–23.
Hollway, W. (1991) *Work Psychology and Organizational Behaviour*. London: Sage. Chapters 6 and 7 (job satisfaction, training and organisational change).
Miner, J.B. (1992) *Industrial–Organizational Psychology*. New York: McGraw-Hill. Chapter 5 (job satisfaction).
Riggio, R.E. (1999) *Introduction to Industrial and Organizational Psychology (3rd ed)*. Upper Saddle River, NJ: Prentice Hall. Chapter 8 (job satisfaction and QWL), Chapter 9 (stress and burnout).

## Websites

http://www.redmole.co.uk/js_questionnaire/
Reed.co.uk's own questionnaire, the Job Satisfaction Index – fill it in and get feedback immediately! (That's Reed Employment).

http://catalogue.bized.ac.uk/roads/persat.html
Bized's site for job satisfaction and QWL.

http://www.stress.org.uk/Index.htm
A site for those interested in stress in employment. Lots of news,
    questionnaires and further resources/links.

# eight Organisational work conditions

## Introduction

In the last chapter we looked at the issue of stress and how that can directly affect a person's satisfaction with their job and also their productivity and effectiveness in their job. In this chapter we shall consider some of the factors that are likely to lead to stress but also to deterioration of performance level and quality of working life. These sources of discomfort, and even danger, can be listed as:

- Physical and psychological conditions of work environments: physical factors such as noise, pollution, temperature, illumination; psychological factors such as crowding, personal space and privacy
- Temporal conditions of work environments: the nature of the working day, shift-work, flexitime and so on
- Ways to reduce these negative factors to improve individuals' quality of working life.

## Physical conditions of work environments

### NOISE

It is not just loud noise that will distract a person from work. This is a situation where we must consider individual differences as well as sheer intensity of noise. Some people are distracted by any sound at all while others can, for instance, study for examinations with the radio blaring away. Nevertheless there are some absolute levels of sound that will necessarily be physically damaging. A quiet office measures about 40 decibels of sound, an average factory area 100, a pneumatic hammer 130 and a jet plane at take-off 150. Continuous exposure to these higher levels has been linked to such stress-related symptoms as ulcers and high blood pressure (Evans *et al*., 1995; Nagar and Panady, 1987) and will inevitably lead to incurable hearing loss. You will notice nowadays that at airports and on construction sites workers often wear headphone silencers attached to safety helmets. A wide range of studies on the effects of noise has been conducted and overall conclusions are that:

- Noise problems can be indirectly related to safety and health as communications are made more difficult and it is harder to pick up feedback from one's machine.
- Noise affects error more than it lowers performance.
- High-pitched noise interferes with performance more than low-pitched noise (Riggio, 1999).

Loudness of noise is not always the problem. Graig (1993) showed that people were bothered most by noises that were new, intermittent or unpredictable. Some research has shown that although noise affects difficult tasks requiring concentration, it can actually *increase* performance on boring repetitive tasks (Sanders and McCormick, 1987). Thinking back to Chapter 7 where we discussed stress caused by *lack* of stimulation, this is understandable as many people feel the need for noise stimulation in the form of music in order to perform dull tasks like painting a wall or motorway driving. Most office workers view background music favourably (Sundstrom, 1986 in Riggio).

ILLUMINATION AND VISION

Although we shall look briefly at the negative effects on performance of poor lighting it is worth referring here to a famous set of studies described in the following Theme link box.

In general, the better the illumination the better the performance, especially for tasks involving fine visual discrimination (Sanders and McCormick, 1993). However, even for increasing light there is a limit at which, depending on the type of task, performance deteriorates. You may have wondered why schools, offices and commercial premises use fluorescent lighting. This is because such lighting is better distributed and produces greater illumination at lower cost.

Glare is a particular problem for some tasks, as any driver who has faced opposing headlights on a dark country road will know. Ways to protect against this in the workplace are the use of goggles or shields and making bright surfaces matt in order to diffuse any reflected light.

A contemporary concern has been the complaints of fatigue, headaches and eye strain emanating from people who work in front of a computer screen for large parts of each day. To alleviate these symptoms employers have introduced screen filters that reduce glare.

In the late 1920s and early 1930s a series of studies was carried out at the Western Electrical Company's 'Hawthorne' site in Chicago, USA (Roethlisberger and Dickson, 1939). At first the researchers were interested in the simple effects of varying physical conditions such as illumination and work/rest hours.

In one now classic experiment, (Mayo, 1927 cited in Rose, 1975) the light was varied for a group of female workers who assembled telephone relays. These workers were moved to a separate test room where their performance was carefully measured. To the researchers' amazement, productivity tended to increase whatever change was made to the lighting level, with detriment occurring only when the workers were in very deep gloom. The research team concluded that factors more social in nature were responsible for the increases in productivity and the very high morale among employees. These studies were instrumental in developing the view that workers are not just machines, but have feelings and attitudes at work and about work which are very much affected by social conditions. The name **Hawthorne effect** is now given to the idea in general that in any psychological investigation, where people know that an outcome is expected, results can be contaminated by the fact that participants may behave according to these expectations. The Hawthorne workers appeared to increase productivity no matter what the experimental variable. It seemed only that they were fulfilling the researchers' expectations of them.

However a word of caution is in order from the view of clear, well controlled studies. Gregory (1987) writes that:

> It was generally considered that the increase was due to social factors within the group, although it could be accounted for by the change in group piece-work which was shared among a group of five instead of a larger group, the smaller variety of work done, the replacement of two of the girls by faster ones, the enthusiasm of the penurious operative number two, and the general expectation throughout the works that the experiment would be a 'success'. (p.303)

Any one of these variables that also changed with the lighting level could have confounded the results and therefore could have been the effective cause of the productivity increases.

## TEMPERATURE

When I travelled in Kuwait I was amazed to see bare-backed workers out digging roads in temperatures of 40 degrees centigrade, while I wilted just sitting in a coach. Personally I have worked in fairly cold conditions – on a milk round collecting bottles in sub-zero temperatures and in an ice-cream loading depot. Common sense tells me I was not performing at my best. Research tells us that the Kuwaiti workers too were probably performing well below par since both manual and cognitive performance decrease above 32 degrees centigrade (Kobrick and Fine, 1983) and an optimum working temperature is around 22 degrees. High humidity particularly inhibits heavy physical work while, not surprisingly, very low temperatures inhibit fine motor movements, as anyone trying to untie their boot laces after a freezing walk will know. However, most research is conducted in the laboratory setting and therefore it is difficult to know what specific effects temperature has under the influence of the many variables, including individual differences, which may be operating in the work place.

### other senses

Contrary to popular opinion, there is little supportive research evidence for the notion that certain colours have more positive effects on work performance. However there is fascinating research reported by Baron and Bronfen (1994) showing positive effects on motivation and work attitudes, and a lowering of conflict, when air fresheners were used to create a pleasant smell! Before employers rush to scent the workplace it should be noted that this was only a *simulated* work environment, but the area is ripe for further naturalistic study.

### pollution

A whole raft of factors have been discovered over the years which seriously affect workers' health. Miners we now know are particularly susceptible to pneumacosis, and asbestos workers succumbed to a wide-ranging variety of cancers until the substance was banned for building purposes. Asbestos discovered in houses now is removed by highly specialised personnel wearing protective clothing. Carbon monoxide poisoning causes a decrease in attention, memory, co-ordination and problem-solving ability and is therefore a risk for anyone working outside, near congested traffic or running engines.

### repetitive work

We saw in the last chapter that repetitive jobs are the least satisfying and are associated with high levels of stress-related symptoms. As long ago as 1937, Barmack showed that assembly-line work that is boring and monotonous can decrease physiological arousal and is associated with negative attitudes towards work.

# Psychological conditions of the work environment

## SPACE

The layout of a work area can be of great importance to an individual employee. People will fight quite hard to achieve the goal of a personal office. At my university recently academics in one department were threatened with a change of building that would have entailed many staff moving from their own single offices to a room containing five tutors. Not only was this a threat in terms of status, but various other serious psychological effects were outlined during discussion of the move. How was research to be conducted when four other people were entering, leaving and using the room? How were students to talk to their tutors in confidence? How were tutors to concentrate on what students were discussing with them while four other staff could listen, or were having a discussion, or were making tea? Interestingly, the senior manager with overall responsibility for the proposed move enjoyed a very large, private office with a panoramic view, yet found it hard to understand the reactions of the academic staff.

While **open plan offices** permit social interaction and can improve worker satisfaction, over-congestion and an excess of socialising can impair work performance (Canter, 1983). Research gives mixed results and shows that open plan offices may increase informal conversations whilst not improving formal communication; lack of confidentiality may violate personal privacy (Sundstrom, 1986). Workers in open plan offices report double the number of headaches reported by other office workers (Hedge, 1984).

Preference for open plan or closed offices will depend upon the status of the worker and the type of task in which they are involved. Managers and similar level workers tend to dislike open plan probably because of the implied loss of status (Werner and Haggard, 1992). Tutors and counsellors, whose job requires privacy, probably cannot work effectively in an open plan environment. People working on complex tasks requiring concentration also prefer closed offices (Block and Stokes, 1989).

The factor of office space has been considered as part of the overall phenomenon known as **sick building syndrome**. British gas opted for open plan offices at their new headquarters in the UK and soon after experienced a significant rise in absenteeism and a deterioration in performance and motivation. Probably several factors were involved but the whole issue of building design for the workplace came into question (see Coolican *et al.*, 1996).

## crowding

Closely related to the factor of space is that of **crowding**. Generally, the more people who work around you the more likely you are to experience stress (Weiss and Baum, 1987). Oldham and Fried (1987) found that employee satisfaction and turnover were related to four interlinked factors: number of co-workers in an office, seating distance between these workers, number of enclosures (e.g. partitions) around each workstation, and overall darkness. Darkness, crowding and few partitions, taken together, made employees more likely to leave.

### psychological stress factors

In Chapter 7 we described various sources of stress at work and these should all be referred to of course when discussing psychological conditions in the work environment.

**Section summary**    Physical conditions which may affect performance include: noise, illumination, temperature, colour, smell, pollution and repetitive work. High-level and intermittent noise can be particularly disruptive. Greater illumination produces better performance within limits and depending on task. Temperatures outside the optimum range tend to weaken performance. Pleasant smells may enhance performance. Psychological conditions include: space, crowding and stressful conditions. Space has a mixture of effects which depend upon task, status and forms of communication. Space, crowding and lighting may have significant effects on satisfaction.

## Temporal conditions of the work environment

Jobs can be performed under a variety of temporal conditions to do with how long and in what time pattern you work. Variations from the standard 9 to 5 involve shift work, part-time work, flexitime (organising your own working hours to some extent), and part working at home. In a study of oil rig employees – who work long periods on the rig then have a long period off – the longer the on-period the greater the related stress (Sutherland and Cooper, 1987). Long hours in general have been found to be less productive and to be more associated with ill-health of various kinds (Sparks and Cooper, 1997 in Arnold *et al.*, 1998).

**Shift work** in general appears to be an unhealthy way to work, which is worrying because modern life demands more of it. Factories can stay open 24 hours because of computerised machinery, people in general are demanding that shops and services become ever more available and many supermarkets in the UK now offer 24-hour shopping. Shift workers generally have lower job satisfaction, lower performance, greater health risks (including cardiovascular disease and gastrointestinal disorders), and more domestic and social problems (Dipboye *et al.* 1994), possibly because of the disruption of circadian rhythms (natural sleep–wake cycles). Accident rates appear to be higher for late-night shift workers (Schweitzer, Muelbach and Walsh, 1992). Women in particular can end up sleeping far too little because they return to childcare duties during the daytime hours. However, the main complaint of shift workers in the British steel industry (Wedderburn, 1981) was its negative effect on their social life. Sadly, Tepas et al. (1985) found that divorce was 50 per cent more frequent among night workers than other groups.

Many factors may confound the shift work findings. For instance, perhaps those who are less suited to married life are also those who are more attracted to shift work and the freedoms it also permits, thus accounting for some of the higher divorce rate.

**Flexitime** gives the employee more control over their working hours; they may come in an hour earlier or later and leave earlier or later as a consequence. Little data exist on the effects of this approach but Dalton and Mesch (1990) showed it to be related to lower absenteeism. Most studies appear to show that neither performance nor satisfaction are improved but that workers are keen on the programmes probably partly because of the perceived control over work that they gain (Dipboye et al., 1994). Satisfaction, but not performance, was found to be improved among workers on a **compressed working week** – for example four ten-hour days per week (Di Milia, 1998 cited in Riggio, 1999).

Flexitime is of increasing importance in the debate about equal opportunities for women at work. For instance, allowing either parent to take children to school before starting work relieves the traditional pressure on women who are otherwise disadvantaged in the types of job they can take or the promotion they can expect. Similarly, working extra hours some days permits a parent to collect children from school on others and avoid expensive childcare fees.

> **Section summary**
>
> The phrase 'temporal conditions' refers to the pattern of working hours and days for a particular worker. Various negative job attitudes and health risks are associated with shift work. Causes are various but could include conflicts with domestic duties, disruption of sleep cycles and possibly the attraction of only certain types of people into this pattern. Long hours affect performance and longer spells working away increase stress. Flexitime patterns are popular and compressed weeks are related to satisfaction.

# Reducing the negative effects of work environments for individuals

The reader might like to conduct a mental exercise now: think of all the factors that a sensitive and humanitarian employer might consider when designing a work environment with a view to minimising the negative effects on employees. Table 8.1 opposite summarises several of the steps that can be taken to minimise the effects of environmental factors. In addition to these, and in general terms, modern organisations can implement *interventions* in the workplace designed to lower the negative impact of work on individuals, in particular the effects of stress. The following types of intervention are possible:

- organisational change (minor or major)
- stress management training
- counselling
- health promotion.

Cooper and Cartwright (1994) argue that most organisations use one or a combination of the last of these three types, collectively known as **employee assistance programmes** (EAPs). Typically organisations find it less expensive to deal with the individual's problems, to help individuals to change, than they do to implement expensive organisational changes such as:

- job redesign (see Chapter 7)
- work environment redesign
- employee participation in decisions and planning
- flexible working schedules
- team building
- overall changes in organisational culture.

This is in line with Tom Cox's claim (2001), mentioned in the Introduction, that so far the majority of applications of occupational and organisational psychology have tended to benefit employers and output, rather than being of overall benefit to the majority of working people. As Arnold *et al.* (1998) point out, EAPs 'present a high-profile means by which organisations can "be seen to doing something about stress" and taking reasonable precautions to safeguard employee health' (p.448).

The evidence on EAPs is mixed. It generally points towards improved mental health but no improvement in job satisfaction or productivity. Reynolds *et al.* (1993) found that **stress management programmes** lowered self-reported stress indicators but did not increase job satisfaction; **workplace**

• **Table 8.1:** The optimum work environment

|  | Reducing negative effects |
|---|---|
| **Physical conditions** | |
| Noise | Keep noise below 90 decibels; staff to wear ear protectors; reduce any intermittent or sudden noises; ensure clear communication above noise; provide visual feedback from machinery where noise might interfere; provide background music especially with boring tasks; adapt to individual differences where possible. |
| Illumination | Provide bright lighting; avoid glare using matt surfaces and computer monitor screens. |
| Temperature | Keep temperature around 22°C. Certainly below 32°C and well above zero! Control humidity. |
| Pollution | Have premises inspected regularly by health and safety personnel; deal instantly with pollution and health risk factors. |
| Repetitive work | Job redesign if possible – see Chapter 7 |
| **Psychological conditions** | |
| Space | Aspects of open plan enough to satisfy social needs for informal discussion but ensure this does not predominate; respect need for privacy in certain roles and status of more senior personnel; closed offices where close concentration or privacy is required. |
| Crowding | Where open plan exists, provide maximum seating distance possible and lowest number of personnel per room; use partitions to provide privacy and keep spaces well lit. |
| Stress | Deal with factors in Table 7.2 by for instance: team building exercises; open flow of information about job status, tenure, changes; redesign jobs; clarify roles and responsibilities; provide stress management and health promotion programmes in organisational time; make more fundamental changes to organisational structure where possible. |
| **Temporal conditions** | |
| Shift work | Allow longer rotation of shifts to permit acclimatisation to circadian rhythms; counsel mature (late 40s+) workers off shift work where possible (since Monk and Folkard, 1985, found mature workers to be more morning-oriented and less flexible in adaptation); attend to other individual differences (e.g. morning types or 'larks' may not work well at night); provide counselling about shift work effects; reduce hours and share out overtime evenly; implement flexitime working. |

**counselling** can lower absenteeism and mental health symptoms but also tends not to increase satisfaction (Cooper and Sadri, 1991). Similarly **health promotion programmes**, in which employees are encouraged to attend health and fitness classes in work time, tend to increase worker health significantly, but much of this may be short-term if individuals do not make a commitment to maintain their new healthy lifestyle.

**Section summary**    Suggestions for dealing with negative physical, psychological and temporal conditions are given in Table 8.1. Organisations can also provide employee assistance programmes (EAPs) and these have been preferred to the perceived greater expense incurred in organisational change to prevent negative conditions and stress in the first place. EAPs include stress management, health promotion and counselling programmes. Such programmes have been shown to have limited effects on absenteeism and employee health but do not tend to improve satisfaction or performance levels.

### KEY TERMS

**compressed working week**
**crowding**
**employee assistance programmes**
**flexitime**
**Hawthorne effect**
**health promotion programmes**
**open plan offices**
**shift work**
**sick building syndrome**
**stress management training**
**temporal conditions**
**workplace counselling**

EXERCISE **1**

If time and other conditions allow, try conducting the following experiment. (This could be run as a practical to be reported for coursework but in this case it would be wiser to stick to just two conditions.) According to research, new and intermittent noises disturb performance more than recognised and regular noises. Have participants perform a relatively complex task such as a numerical test, a crossword or even a revision test in organisational psychology! Use the following conditions:

- regular noise from the start of the experimental instruction giving
- intermittent noise throughout the test period
- a new noise that starts just as the test begins
- control condition with no noise at all.

The noise can be provided by a handily placed food proccssor, electric drill etc. You need an operationalised measure of performance such as number of test answers correct, clues solved, or time taken to complete the test. Compare the performances of the different groups. If possible conduct significance tests between pairs of means, noting that multiple significance tests increase the probability of a Type I error. That is, with more tests you have a greater chance of getting a fluke 'significant' result. However, the main point of the study is the design of the exercise and the inspection of trends in the results which might lead to a more formally organised research experiment. You could also compare performances on simple and complex tasks under these conditions.

EXERCISE 2

Conduct a survey among working people available to you (e.g. friends, relatives, neighbours, staff in your school/college) to find out:

- their attitude towards a four-day working week with a few hours extra per day to compensate
- their attitude towards flexitime
- the extent and type of flexitime available in their employment.

Ensure that your survey uses standardised questions and both quantitative and qualitative response formats. For the quantitative items ensure that the same response scale is used for all respondents and that it produces data that can be sensibly summarised and analysed.

Both these exercises require tutor assistance.

## ESSAY QUESTIONS

1. Discuss the ways in which physical and psychological conditions at work can affect both performance and satisfaction.

2. In what ways can organisations ensure that the temporal conditions under which employees work are organised to produce the best levels of performance and satisfaction?

# Further reading

Riggio, R.E. (1999) *Introduction to Industrial and Organizational Psychology* (3rd ed). Upper Saddle River, NJ: Prentice Hall. Chapter 16.

# Websites

http://www.fastcompany.com/cgi-bin/votato/in.cgi?openplan_a
A new interactive discussion site that requested thoughts on open plan offices. Contains very many e-mails putting personal views on advantages and disadvantages from the sender's own experience.

http://www.nonoise.org/cgi-bin/query.cgi?db=hearing
From the 'Noise Pollution Clearing House' – from here you can go to resources on occupational noise issues and findings in the USA.

http://www.ohsonline.com/
Occupational Health and Society – a US-based on-line magazine on health and safety at work in a social context.

http://www.apa.org/journals/ocp.html
Journal of Occupational Health Psychology – on-line academic journal.

http://www.work-and-health.org/future/map/structure.htm
University of California academic department with information on shift work, useful links and material on stress in general.

# References

Adams, J.S. (1965) Inequity in social exchange. In L. Berkowitz (ed) *Advances in Experimental Social Psychology,* Vol. 2. New York: Academic Press.

Adams, J.S. and Rosenbaum, W.B. (1962) The relationship of worker productivity to cognitive dissonance about wage inequities. *Journal of Applied Psychology,* 46, 161–4.

Agho, A.O., Mueller, C.W. and Price, J.L. (1993) Determinants of employee job satisfaction: An empirical test of a causal model. *Human Relations,* 46, 1007–27.

Alderfer, C.P. (1972) *Organizational Development: Human needs in organizational settings.* New York: Free Press.

Alimo-Metcalf, B. and Alban-Metcalf, R.J. (2000) A new approach to assessing transformational leadership. *Selection and Development Review,* 16, 5, 15–17.

Aronson, E., Bridgeman, D.L. and Geffner, R. (1978) The effects of a cooperative classroom structure on student behaviour and attitudes. In D.Bar-tel and L.Saxe (Eds.), *Social Psychology of Education.* New York: Wiley.

Arnold, J., Cooper, C.L. and Robertson, I.T. (1998) *Work Psychology: Understanding Human Behaviour in the Workplace.* London: Financial Times/Pitman Publishing.

Asch, S. (1956) Studies of independence and conformity: A minority of one against a unanimous majority. *Psychological Monographs,* 70.

Ash, R.A. and Edgell, S.L. (1975) A note on the readability of the Position Analysis Questionnaire (PAQ). *Journal of Applied Psychology,* 60, 765–6.

Awosunle, S. and Doyle, C. (2001) Same-race bias in the selection interview. *Selection Development Review,* 17, 3, 3–6.

Baird, J.E. (1977) *The Dynamics of Organizational Communication.* New York: Harper and Row.

Banks, M.H., Jackson, P.R., Stafford, E.M. and Warr, P.B. (1983) The job components inventory and the analysis of jobs requiring limited skill. *Personnel Psychology,* 36, 57–66.

Barmack, J.E. (1937) Boredom and other factors in the physiology of mental effort: An explanatory study. *Archives of Psychology*, 218, 1–83.

Baron, R.A. and Bronfen, M.I. (1994) A whiff of reality: empirical evidence concerning the effects of pleasant fragrances on work-related behavior. *Journal of Applied Social Psychology*, 24, 1179–1203.

Bartlett, F.C. (1932) *Remembering*. Cambridge: Cambridge University Press.

Bartram, D. and Lindley, P.A. (1994) *Psychological Testing: The BPS Level A Open Learning Programme*. Leicester: BPS.

Bartram, D., Lindley, P.A., Marshall, L. and Foster, J. (1995) The recruitment and selection of young people by small businesses. *Journal of Occupational and Organizational Psychology*, 68, 4, 339–358.

Bass, B.M. (1985) *Leadership and Performance: Beyond expectations*. New York: Free Press.

Bavelas, A. (1969) Communications patterns in task-oriented groups, In Cartwright, D. and Zander, A. (Eds) *Group Dynamics: Research and Theory*, 3rd ed. New York: Harper and Row.

Belbin, R.M. (1993) *Team Role at Work: A strategy for human resource management*. Oxford: Butterworth-Heinemann.

Betz, E.L. (1982) Need fulfillment in the career development of women. *Journal of Vocational Behaviour*, 20, 60–61.

Block, L. and Stokes, G. (1989) Performance and satisfaction in private versus non-private work settings. *Environment and Behaviour*, 21, 277–97.

Bransford, J.D. and Johnson, M.K. (1972) Contextual prerequisites for understanding: Some investigations of comprehension and recall. *Journal of Verbal Learning and Verbal Behavior*, 11, 717–26.

Brown, C. and Gay, P. (1985) *17 Years after the Act*. London: Policy Studies Institute.

Brown, R. (1988) *Group Processes*. Oxford: Blackwell

Bryman, A. (1992) *Charisma and Leadership in Organizations*. London: Sage.

Burns, J.M. (1978) *Leadership*. New York: Harper and Row.

Burt, C. (1924) The mental differences between individuals. *Journal of the National Institute of Industrial Psychology*, 11, 2, 67–74.

Byrne, B.M. (1993) The Maslach Burnout Inventory: Testing for factorial validity and invariance across elementary, intermediate and secondary teachers. *Journal of Occupational and Organizational Psychology*, 66, 197–212.

Campion, M.A., Pursell, E.D. and Brown, B.K. (1988) Structured interviewing: Raising the psychometric properties of the employment interview. *Personnel Psychology*, 41, 25–42.

Canter, D. (1983) The physical context of work. In D.J. Oborne and M.M. Gruneberg (Eds) *The Physical Environment at Work*. Chichester: John Wiley & Sons.

Chmiel, N. (2000) *Work and Organizational Psychology: A European Perspective*. Oxford: Blackwell.

Coolican, H., Cassidy, T., Cherchar, A., Harrower, J., Penny, G., Sharp, R., Walley, M. and Westbury, T. (1996) *Applied Psychology*. London: Hodder & Stoughton.

Cooper, C.L. and Cartwright, S. (1994) Healthy mind; healthy organization – a proactive approach to occupational stress. *Human Relations*, 47, 4, 455–71.

Cooper, M.D., Phillips, R.A., Sutherland, V.J. and Makin, P.J. (1994) Reducing accidents using goal-setting theory and feedback: A field study. *Journal of Occupational and Organizational Psychology*, 67, 219–40.

Cooper, C.L. and Sadri, G. (1991) The impact of stress counselling at work. In P.L. Perrewe (Ed.) *Handbook of Job Stress (Special Issue), Journal of Social Behavior and Personality,* vol 6., no.7., 411–23.

Cox, T. (2001) *'What? Occupational Psychology: Making a Difference'*. Lecture given at British Psychological Society conference: 'Psychology – a Science for Society.' 5th January, 2001 at The Royal Society.

Crutchfield, R.S. (1955) Conformity and character. *American Psychologist*, 10, 191–8.

Cummings, T. and Cooper, C.L. (1979) A cybernetic framework for the study of occupational stress. *Human Relations, 32, 395–419.*

Dalton, D.R. and Mesch, D.J. (1990) The impact of flexible scheduling on employee attendance and turnover. *Administrative Science Quarterly*, 35, 370–87.

Dansereau, F., Graen, G. and Haga, B. (1975) A vertical dyad linkage approach to leadership within formal organizations: A longitudinal investigation of the role making process. *Organizational Behaviour and Human Performance*, 13, 46–78.

de Board, R. (1978) *The Psychoanalysis of Organizations*. London: Tavistock.

Deutsch, M. (1949) An experimental study of the effects of cooperation and competition upon group process. *Human Relations*, 2, 199–231.

Dipboye, R.L., Smith, C.S. and Howell, W.C. (1994) *Understanding Industrial and Organizational Psychology: An integrated approach*. Fort Worth: Harcourt Brace.

Earley, P.C. (1989) Social loafing and collectivism: A comparison of the United States and the People's Republic of China. *Administrative Science Quarterly*, 34, 565–81.

Erez, M. and Somech, A. (1996) Is group productivity loss the rule or the exception? Effects of culture and group-based motivation. *Academy of Management Journal*, 39, 6, 1513–1537.

Evans, G.W., Hygge, S. and Bullinger, M. (1995) Chronic noise and psychological stress. *Psychological Science,* 6, 333–338.

Eysenck, M.W. and Keane, M.T. (1995) *Cognitive Psychology: A student's handbook* (3rd ed). Hove: LEA.

Fiedler, F.E. (1967) *A Theory of Leadership Effectiveness*. New York: McGraw-Hill.

Fiedler, F.E. (1995) Cognitive resources and leadership performance. *Applied Psychology: An international review*, 44, 5–28.

Fine, S.A. (1988) Functional job analysis. In S.Gael (Ed.), *The Job Analysis Handbook for Business, Industry and Government* Vol. 2, 1019–1035. New York: Wiley.

Flanagan, J.C. (1954) The critical incident technique. *Psychological Bulletin*, 51, 327–58.

Fleishman, E.A. (1969) *Leadership Opinion Questionnaire Manual*. Henley-on-Thames: Science Research Associates.

Fletcher, C. (1995) New directions for performance appraisal; Some findings and observations. *International Journal of Selection and Assessment*, 3, 191–6.

Fraser, C., Gouge, C. and Billig, M. (1971) Risky shifts, cautious shifts and group polarisation. *European Journal of Social Psychology*, 1, 7–30.

Friedman, M., and Rosenman, R.H. (1974) *Type A Behaviour and Your Heart*. New York: Alfred A Knopf.

Furnham, A. (1997) *The Psychology of Behaviour at Work*. Hove: Psychology Press.

Ganster, D.C., Schaubroeck, J., Sime, W.E. and Mayes, B.T. (1991) The nomological validity of the Type A personality among employed adults. *Journal of Applied Psychology*, 76, 143–68.

Gold, M. A. (2000) Pygmalion in cyberspace: Leaders' high expectancies for subordinate performance conveyed electronically versus face-to-face. *Dissertation Abstracts International Section B: Sciences and Engineering*, 61, 4-B, 2255.

Gotcher, J. M. (1997) Perceptions and uses of electronic mail: A function of rhetorical style. *Social Science Computer Review*, 15, 2, 145–158.

Graig, E. (1993) Stress as a consequence of the urban physical environment. In L. Goldberg and S. Breznitz (Eds.) *Handbook of Stress: Theoretical and clinical aspects.* (2nd. Ed) New York: Free Press.

Graves, L.M. and Powell, G.N. (1996) Sex similarity, quality of the employment interview and recruiters' evaluation of actual applicants. *Journal of Occupational and Organisational Psychology*, 69, 243–61.

Gregory, R.L. (Ed.) (1987) *The Oxford Companion to the Mind*. Oxford: Oxford University Press.

Hackman, J.R. and Oldham, G.R. (1975) Development of the Job Diagnostic Survey. *Journal of Applied Psychology*, 60, 159–70.

Hackman, J.R. and Oldham, G.R. (1976) Motivation through the design of work: Test of a theory. *Organisational Behaviour and Human Performance*, 16, 250–279.

Hedge, A. (1984) Ill health among office workers: An examination of the relationship between office design and employee well-being. In E.Grandjean (Ed.) *Ergonomics and Health in Modern Offices*. London:

Taylor and Francis.

Herzberg, F. (1966) *Work and the Nature of Man*. Cleveland: World Publishing.

Hollenbeck, J.R. Williams, C.R. and Klein, H.J. (1989) An empirical examination of the antecedents of commitment to difficult goals. *Journal of Applied Psychology*, 74, 18–23.

Hollway, W. (1991) *Work Psychology and Organizational Behaviour*. London: Sage.

House, R.J. (1977) A 1976 theory of charismatic leadership. In J.G. Hunt and L.L. Larson (Eds) *Leadership: The cutting edge*. Carbondale, IL: Southern Illinois Press.

House, R.J., Spangler, W.D. and Woycke, J. (1991) Personality and charisma in the US presidency: A psychological theory of leadership effectiveness. *Administrative Science Quarterly*, 36, 364–96.

Huffcut, A.I. and Arthur, W.A. (1994) Hunter and Hunter revisited: Interview validity for entry-level jobs. *Journal of Applied Psychology*, 79, 184–90.

Hunter, J.E. and Hunter, R.F. (1984) Validity and utility of alternative predictors of job performance. *Psychological Bulletin*, 96, 72–98.

Ilgen, D.R. and Klein, H.J. (1989) Organizational behaviour. *Annual Review of Psychology*, 40, 327–51.

Janis, I.L. (1972) *Victims of Groupthink: A Psychological Study of Foreign-policy Decisions and Fiascoes*. Boston: Houghton Mifflin.

Johnson, D.W., Maruyama, G., Johnson, R., Nelson, D. and Skon, L. (1981) Effects of co-operative, competitive and individualistic goal structures on achievement: A meta-analysis. *Psychological Bulletin*, 89, 1, 47–62.

Kabanoff, B. (1985) Potential influence structures as sources of interpersonal conflict in groups and organizations, *Organizational Behaviour and Human Decision Processes*, 36, 113–141.

Kline, P. (1993) *The Handbook of Psychological Testing*. London: Routledge.

Knoke, D. and Wright-Isak, C. (1982) Individual motives and organisational incentive systems. *Research in the Sociology of Organisations*, 1, 209–54.

Kobrick, J.L. and Fine, B.J. (1983) Climate and human performance. In D.J. Oborne and M.M. Gruneberg (Eds) *The Physical Environment at Work* Chichester: John Wiley & Sons.

Koehler, J.W., Anatol, K.W.E. and Applbaum, R.L. (1981) *Organizational Communication: Behavioral Perspectives* (2nd ed). New York: Holt, Rinehart and Winston.

Kranzusch, M.J. (1997) The effect of extrinsic and intrinsic reward systems on employee motivation. *Dissertation Abstracts International Section A: Humanities and Social Sciences*, July, 58 (1-A).

Kunin, T. (1955) The construction of a new type of attitude measure. *Personnel Psychology*, 8, 65–77.

Landy, F.J. (1985) *Psychology of Work Behaviour*. Chicago, IL: The Doesey Press.

Larsen, H.H. and Bang, S.M. (1993) Development dialogues as an alternative to performance appraisal: A tool for strategic human resource development in Europe. *Research in Personnel and Human Resource Management*, Supplement 3, 171–88.

Latham, G.P., Erez, M. and Locke, E.A. (1988) Resolving scientific disputes by the joint design of crucial experiments by the antagonists: Application to the Latham-Erez dispute regarding participation in goal setting. *Journal of Applied Psychology*, 73, 753–72.

Latham, G.P. and Saari, L.M. (1984) Do people do what they say? Further studies on the situational interview. *Journal of Applied Psychology*, 69, 569–73.

Leavitt, H.J. (1951) Some effects of certain communication patterns on group performance. *Journal of Abnormal and Social Psychology*, 46, 38–50.

Leiter, M.P. and Maslach, C. (1988) The impact of interpersonal environment on burnout and organizational commitment. *Journal of Organizational Behaviour*, 9, 297–308.

Lengel, R.H. and Daft, R.L. (1988) The selection of communication media as an executive skill. *The Academy of Management Executives*, 11, 225–32.

Leon, F.R. (1981) The role of positive and negative outcomes in the causation of motivational forces. *Journal of Applied Psychology*, 66, 45–53.

Lewin, K., Lippitt, R. And White, R. (1939) Patterns of aggressive behaviour in experimentally created 'social climates'. *Journal of Social Psychology*, 10, 271–99.

Lewthwaite-Patel, A. (2001) 360 degree feedback: A user's perspective. *Selection Development Review*, 17, 2, 6–9.

Locke, E.A. and Latham, G.P. (1990) *A Theory of Goal-setting and Task Performance*. Englewood Cliffs, NJ: Prentice Hall.

Locke, E.A., Shaw, K.N., Saari, L.M. and Latham, G.P. (1981) Goal setting and task performance 1969–1980. *Psychological Bulletin*, 90, 125–52.

Locke, J. L. (1998) *The De-voicing of Society: Why we don't talk to each other anymore*. New York: Simon and Schuster.

Loher, B.T., Noe, R.A. Moeller, N.L. and Fitzgerald, M.P. (1985) A meta-analysis of the relation of job characteristics to job satisfaction. *Journal of Applied Psychology*, 70, 280–9.

McClelland, D.C. (1961) *The Achieving Society*. Princeton, NJ: Van Nostrand.

McCormick, E.J., Jeanneret, P.R. and Meacham, R.C. (1972) A study of job characteristics and Job dimensions as based on the Position Analysis Questionnaire (PAQ). *Journal of Applied Psychology*, 56, 347–68.

Maier, N.R.F. and Solem, A.R. (1952) The contribution of a discussion leader to the quality of group thinking: The effective use of minority opinions. *Human Relations*, 5, 277–88.

Maslow, A. (1954) *Motivation and Personality*. New York: Harper and Row.

Meade, R.D. (1967) An experimental study of leadership in India. *Journal of*

*Social Psychology*, 72, 35–43.

Minard, R.D. (1952) Race relationships in the Pocahontas Coal Field. *Journal of Social Issues*, 8, 29–44

Miner, J.B. (1992) *Industrial–Organizational Psychology*. New York: McGraw-Hill.

Moghaddam, F.M. (1998) *Social Psychology: Exploring universals across cultures*. New York: Freeman.

Monk, T.H. and Folkard, S. (1985) Shiftwork and performance. In S. Folkard and T. Monk (Eds) *Hours of Work: Temporal factors in work-scheduling*. Chichester: Wiley.

Moscovici, S. (1985) Social influence and conformity. In G. Lindzey and A. Aronson (Eds) *The Handbook of Social Psychology*, 3rd ed. New York: Random House.

Muchinsky, P.M. (1977) Organizational communication: Relationships to organizational climate and job satisfaction. *Academy of Management Journal*, 20, 592–607.

Nagar, D. and Panady, J. (1987) Affect and performance on cognitive tasks as a function of crowding and noise. *Journal of Applied Social Psychology*, 17, 147–57.

Nemeth, C.J. (1986) Differential contributions of majority and minority influence. *Psychological Review*, 93, 23–32.

O'Reilly, C.A. (1980) Individuals and information overload in organizations: Is more necessarily better? *Academy of Management Journal*, 23, 684–96.

Oldham, G.R. and Fried, Y. (1987) Employee reactions to work space characteristics. *Journal of Applied Psychology*, 72, 75-80.

Peters, L.H., Hartke, D.D and Pohlmann, J.T. (1985) Fiedler's contingency theory of leadership: An application of the meta analysis procedures of Schmidt and Hunter. *Psychological Bulletin*, 97, 274–85.

Radford, J. (2000) Payment to academic authors. *Newsletter of the division for teachers and researchers in Psychology*, 4.

Reynolds, S., Taylor, E. and Shapiro, D.A. (1993) Session impact in stress management training. *Journal of Occupational and Organizational Psychology*, 66, 99–113.

Riggio, R.E. (1990) *Introduction to Industrial and Organizational Psychology*. Glenview, IL: Scott, Foresman & Co.

Riggio, R.E. (1999) *Introduction to Industrial and Organizational Psychology*. (3rd ed) Upper Saddle River, NJ: Prentice Hall.

Roberts, G.E. (1994) Maximising performance appraisal systems effectiveness: Perspectives from municipal government administrators. *Public Personnel Management*, 23, 4, 525–49.

Roberts, K. and Glick, W. (1981) The job characteristics approach to task design: A critical review. *Journal of Applied Psychology*, 66, 193–217.

Rodgers, R. and Hunter, J.E. (1991) Impact of management by objectives on organizational productivity. *Journal of Applied Psychology*, 76, 322–36.

Roethlisberger, F.J. and Dickson, W.J. (1939) *Management and the Worker*, Cambridge, MA: Harvard University Press.

Rollinson, D., Broadfield, A. and Edwards, D.J. (1998) *Organizational Behaviour and Analysis*. Harlow: Addison-Wesley.

Rose, M. (1975) *Industrial behaviour: Theoretical Developments since Taylor*. Harmondsworth: Penguin.

Saks, M.J. and Krupat, E. (1988) *Social Psychology and its Applications*. New York: Harper and Row.

Sanders, M.S. and McCormick, E.J. (1987) *Human factors in engineering and design*. (6th Ed) New York: McGraw-Hill.

Sanders, M.S. and McCormick, E.J. (1993) *Human factors in engineering and design*. (7th Ed) New York: McGraw-Hill.

Scandura, T.A. and Graen, G.B. (1984) Moderating effects of initial leader–member exchange status on the effects of a leadership intervention. *Journal of Applied Psychology*, 69, 428–36.

Schmidt, F.L., Mack, M.J. and HunterJ.E. (1984) Selection utility in the occupation of US Park Ranger for three modes of test use. *Journal of Applied Psychology*, 69, 490–7.

Schriesheim, C.A., Tepper, B.J. and Tetrault, L.A. (1994) Least preferred co-worker score, situational control and leadership effectiveness: A meta-analysis of contingency model performance predictions. *Journal of Applied Psychology*, 79, 561–73.

Schwab, D.P., Olian-Gottlieb, J.D. and Heneman, H.G. (1979) Between subjects expectancy theory research: A statistical review of studies predicting effort and performance. *Psychological Bulletin*, 86, 139–47.

Schweitzer, P.K., Muehlbach, M.J. and Walsh, J.K. (1992) Countermeasures for night work performance deficits: The effect of napping and caffeine on continuous performance at night. *Work and Stress*, 6, 355–65.

Selye, H. [1956] *The Stress of Life*. New York: McGraw-Hill.

Sherif, M., Harvey, O.J., White, B.J., Hood, W.R. and Sherif, C. (1961) *Intergroup Cooperation and Competition: The robbers cave experiment*. Norman, OH: University of Oklahoma.

SHL (1988) *The Work Profiling System*. Thames Ditton: Saville and Holdsworth Ltd.

Skinner, B.F. (1953) *Science and Human Behaviour*. New York: Macmillan.

Smith, F. (1976) Index of Organizational Reaction (IOR). *JSAS Catalogue of Selected Documents in Psychology*, 6, 54, 1265.

Smith, M.J. (1985) Machine-paced work and stress. In C.L.Cooper and M.J.Smith (Eds.) *Job Stress and Blue Collar Work*. Chichester: Wiley.

Smith, P.C., Kendall, L.M. and Hulin, C.L. (1969) *The Measurement of*

*Satisfaction in Work and Retirement.* Chicago, IL: Rand-McNally.

Sparks, K., Cooper, C., Fried, Y. and Shirom, A. (1997) The effects of hours of work on health: A meta-analytic review. Cited in Arnold, J., Cooper, C. and Robertson, I.T. (1998) *Understanding Human Behaviour in the Workplace.* London: Financial Times/Pitman Publishing.

Stagner, R. and Eflal, B. (1982) Internal union dynamics during a strike: A quasi-experimental study. *Journal of Applied and Social Psychology*, 51, 695–6.

Stone, N. (2001) Designing effective study environments. *Journal of Environmental Psychology*, 21, 2, 179–90.

Stoner, J.A.F. (1961) *A comparison of individual and group decisions involving risk.* Unpublished M.A. dissertation. Cambridge: M.I.T.

Sundstrom, E. (1986) *Work Places: The psychology of the physical environment in offices and factories.* Cambridge: Cambridge University Press.

Sutherland, V. and Cooper, C.L. (1987) *Man and Accidents Offshore.* London: Lloyd's.

Tajfel, H., Flament, C., Billig, M.G. and Bundy, R.P. (1971) Social categorization and intergroup behaviour. *European Journal of Social Psychology*, 1, 149–78.

Tepas, D.J., Armstrong, D.R., Carlson, M.L., Duchon, J.C., Gersten, A. and Lezotte, D.V. (1985) Changing industry to continuous operations: Different strokes for different plants. *Behavior Research Methods Instruments and Computers*, 17, 670–6.

Tiene, D. (2000) Online discussions: A survey of advantages and disadvantages compared to face-to-face discussions. *Journal of Educational Multimedia and Hypermedia*, 9, 4, 371–384.

Triandis, H.C. (1994) *Culture and Social Behavior*. New York: McGraw-Hill.

Trist, E.A. and Bamforth, K.W. (1951) Some social and psychological consequences of the Longwall method of coal-getting. *Human Relations*, 4, 3–38.

Vroom, V.H. (1964) *Work and Motivation.* Chichester: John Wiley.

Vroom, V.H. and Jago, A.G. (1988) *The New Leadership: Managing Participation in Organizations.* Englewood Cliffs, NJ: Prentice Hall.

Vroom, V.H. and Yetton, P.W. (1973) *Leadership and Decision-making.* Pittsburgh: Pittsburgh Press.

Wall, T.D. (1982) Perspectives on job redesign. In J.E. Kelly and C.W. Clegg (Eds) *Autonomy and Control in the Workplace.* London: Croom Helm.

Watanabe, N. (2000) Workplace computerization and employee adjustment in Japan. *International Medical Journal*, 7, 1, 17–21.

Wedderburn, A. (1981) Is there a pattern in the value of time off work? In A. Reinberg, N. Vieux and P. Andlaur (Eds.) *Night and Shift Work: Biological and Social Aspects.* Oxford: Pergamon.

Weiss, L. and Baum, A. (1987) Physiological aspects of environment–behavior relationships. In E. Zube and G. Morre (Eds.) *Advances in Environmental Psychology* (Vol. 1). New York: Plenum.

Werner, C.M. and Haggard, L.M. (1992) Avoiding intrusions at the office: Privacy regulation on typical and high solitude days. *Basic and Applied Social Psychology*, 13, 181–93.

Wiesner, W.H. and Cronshaw, S.F. (1988) The moderating impact of interview format and degree of structure on interview validity. *Journal of Occupational Psychology*, 61, 275–290.

Wright, T.A. and Cropanzano, R. (1998) Emotional exhaustion as a predictor of job performance and voluntary turnover. *Journal of Applied Psychology*, 83, 486–493.

# Index